CULTURES OF THE WORLD

Sweden

Cavendish
Square

New York

Published in 2015 by Cavendish Square Publishing, LLC
243 5th Avenue, Suite 136, New York, NY 10016

CPSIA Compliance Information: Batch #WW15CSQ
All websites were available and accurate when this book was sent to press.

Library of Congress Cataloging-in-Publication Data
Gofen, Ethel, 1937-
 Sweden / Ethel Caro Gofen, Leslie Jermyn, Debbie Nevins.
  pages cm. — (Cultures of the world)
 Includes bibliographical references and index.
 ISBN 978-1-50260-074-5 (hardcover) ISBN 978-1-50260-065-3 (ebook)
 1. Sweden—Juvenile literature. I. Jermyn, Leslie. II. Nevins, Debbie. III. Title.
 DL609.G64 2015
 948.5—dc23

                          2014034103

Writers, Ethel Caro Gofen, Leslie Jermyn; Debbie Nevins, third edition
Editor, third edition: Debbie Nevins
Art Director, third edition: Jeffrey Talbot
Designer, third edition: Jessica Nevins
Production Manager, third edition: Jennifer Ryder-Talbot
Cover Picture Researcher: Amy Greenan
Picture Researcher, third edition: Jessica Nevins

PICTURE CREDITS
The photographs in this book are used with the permission of: BMJ/Shutterstock.com, 1; David Thyberg/Moment Open/Getty Images, 3; anse/Shutterstock.com, 5; Muriel Lasure/Shutterstock.com, 6; Antony McAulay/Shutterstock.com, 7; ROBIN HALLDERT/AFP/Getty Images, 8; Conny Sjostrom/Shutterstock.com, 9; BMJ/Shutterstock.com, 10; Andreas Hoynala/iStock/Thinkstock, 34; V. Belov/Shutterstock.com, 13; Tony Johansson/iStock/Thinkstock, 14; Sander van der Werf/Shutterstock.com, 15; PinkBadger/iStock/Thinkstock, 16; Foto_by_M/iStock/Thinkstock, 17; BMJ/Shutterstock.com, 18; Mats Lindberg/iStock/Thinkstock, 19; Veronika Galkina/Shutterstock.com, 20; Rolf_52/Shutterstock.com, 21; Werner Forman/Universal Images Group/Getty Images, 22; sosobuzuk/iStock/Thinkstock, 24; blojfo/Shutterstock.com, 25; Stefan Holm/Shutterstock.com, 26; Dan Koehl/Stockholm bloodbath 1520 greyscale.jpg/Wikimedia Commons, 27; Alexandru Babo Albabos/Kalmar slott.nordostra sidan/Wikimedia Commons, 28; Borisb17/Shutterstock.com, 29; YQHcCAIn9SeBDg at Google Cultural Institute/Attributed to Gustaf L Lundberg - Gustav III, King of Sweden 1772-1792, in a Gustavus Adolphus inspired dress - Google Art Project.jpg/Wikimedia Commons, 30; Photos.com/Thinkstock, 31; IBL Bildbyra/Heritage Images/Getty Images, 33; Derek Berwin/Fox Photos/Hulton Archive/Getty Images, 34; SVEN NACKSTRAND/AFP/Getty Images, 35; TTphoto/Shutterstock.com, 36; Borisb17/iStock/Thinkstock, 37; Luca Teuchmann/WireImage/Getty Images, 38; Geert Koolen/Shutterstock.com, 39; Ivan da Silva/Getty Images, 40; JONATHAN NACKSTRAND/AFP/Getty Images, 41; katatonia82/iStock/Thinkstock, 42; L.H. Roos/Lars August Mannerheim Bex.jpg/Wikimedia Commons, 43; JONATHAN NACKSTRAND/AFP/Getty Images, 44; Monkey Business Images/Shutterstock.com, 46; Kristian Helgesen/Bloomberg/Getty Images, 48; Fedor Selivanov/Shutterstock.com, 50; Esaias BAITEL/Gamma-Rapho/Getty Images, 51; Paolo Bona/Shutterstock.com, 52; JESSICA GOW/AFP/Getty Images, 52; Joakim Lloyd Raboff/Shutterstock.com, 53; Bildagentur Zoonar GmbH/Shutterstock.com, 54; Jamen Percy/Shutterstock.com, 56; Jamen Percy/Shutterstock.com, 57; BMJ/Shutterstock.com, 58; TT/iStock/Thinkstock, 59; Imfoto/Shutterstock.com, 60; BMJ/Shutterstock.com, 62; Elena Pominova/Shutterstock.com, 64; Imfoto/Shutterstock.com, 65; Mark Hannaford/AWL Images/Getty Images, 66; JONATHAN NACKSTRAND/AFP/Getty Images, 67; Conny Sjostrom/Shutterstock.com, 68; Casper Hedberg/Bloomberg/Getty Images, 69; FREDRIK SANDBERG/AFP/Getty Images, 70; Melanie Stetson Freeman/The Christian Science Monitor/Getty Images, 72; JONATHAN NACKSTRAND/AFP/Getty Images, 74; Melanie Stetson Freeman/The Christian Science Monitor/Getty Images, 75; JONATHAN NACKSTRAND/AFP/Getty Images, 77; BMJ/Shutterstock.com, 78; Conny Sjostrom/Shutterstock.com, 80; Peter Isotalo/Storkyrkan2.jpg/Wikimedia Commons, 82; vichie81/Shutterstock.com, 83; Xauxa Håkan Svensson/Heliga Birgitta-den portrattlika.jpg/Wikimedia Commons, 84; JONATHAN NACKSTRAND/AFP/Getty Images, 85; Andrei Nekrassov/Shutterstock.com, 86; Berig/Detail from G 181.jpg/Wikimedia Commons, 87; Olaus Magnus/The Alphabet of the Geats.jpg/Wikimedia Commons, 88; Dusica Paripovic/Moment Open/Getty Images, 89; Sander van der Werf/Shutterstock.com, 91; Pressens Bild/AFP/Getty Images, 92; Alexei Novikov/Shutterstock.com, 93; Melanie Stetson Freeman/The Christian Science Monitor/Getty Images, 94; Peter Bischoff/Getty Images, 95; Rolf_52/Shutterstock.com, 97; Albert L. Ortega/WireImage/Getty Images, 98; JONATHAN NACKSTRAND/AFP/Getty Images, 99; The Print Collector/Print Collector/Getty Images, 100; Banner/Shutterstock.com, 101; Lisa-Lisa/Shutterstock.com 102; Sander van der Werf/Shutterstock.com, 104; sodapix sodapix/Thinkstock, 105; Julian Finney/Getty Images, 106; JONATHAN NACKSTRAND/AFP/Getty Images, 107; Jens Ottoson/Shutterstock.com, 108; TTphoto/Shutterstock.com, 109; Piotr Wawrzyniuk/Shutterstock.com, 110; Bo Jansson/Folio Images/Getty Images, 111; Anna-Mari West/Shutterstock.com, 112; Johner Images/Johner Images/Getty Images, 114; Imfoto/Shutterstock.com, 115; Piotr Wawrzyniuk/Shutterstock.com, 116; SVEN NACKSTRAND/AFP/Getty Images, 117; rQGrnUpToLlIA at Google Cultural Institute /Fanny Brate A Day of Celebration Google Art Project.jpg/Wikimedia Commons, 119; bhofack2/iStock/Thinkstock, 120; Jonas Bergsten/Vaccinium vitis-idaea 20060824 003.jpg/Wikimedia Commons, 121; AnneMS/Shutterstock.com, 122; eugena-klykova/iStock/Thinkstock, 123; gunnargren/Shutterstock.com, 125; Tupungato/Shutterstock.com, 126; Mikael Damkier/Shutterstock.com, 127; Agnes Kantaruk/Shutterstock.com, 128; Nanisimova/Shutterstock.com, 130; vera-g/Shutterstock.com, 131, Banknotes.com, 135.

PRECEDING PAGE
A girl wears the national costume with a flower wreath.

Printed in the United States of America

CONTENTS

SWEDEN TODAY

BY ANY NUMBER OF MEASURES, SWEDEN IS ONE OF THE MOST successful countries in the world. Swedes are among the happiest, healthiest, best educated, safest, greenest (environmentally), and most equal—in terms of gender and social status—of people. The land itself is beautiful, clean, and full of life-giving water. But it is awfully far north, and most people would agree that Sweden's long, gray, snowy winters are one big factor that keeps this country from getting all As on its report card. Of course, winter sports enthusiasts might disagree; others might say the long winter simply makes a Swedish summer all the sweeter.

And Swedes do love summer. With its bountiful wild strawberries, long days of endless sun, and mild, Gulf Stream—warmed climate, summer in Sweden is welcomed with a flower-bedecked festival of singing, dancing, feasting, and drinking, with enough merrymaking to make anyone forget winter. The Swedish government gets in the spirit as well, granting working people an abundant number of vacation days in which to enjoy the season—a whopping forty-one days a year (twenty-five paid vacation days and sixteen paid holidays), which puts Sweden at the very top of the world's most paid vacation list.

Swedes love the great outdoors.

With everyone lazing around in hammocks, one might think Sweden's economy is going nowhere fast, but just the opposite is true. The World Economic Forum ranks Sweden the sixth most economically competitive country in the world. Most people work, and most people who want jobs have jobs. About 74 percent of Swedes age fifteen to sixty-four are employed, with long-term unemployment statistics being quite low at 1.4 percent. Unlike in some countries, Sweden's working population tends to labor a reasonable number of hours, with only 1 percent of people working more than fifty hours a week. This allows Swedes to enjoy a healthy work-life balance that contributes to physical and mental well-being—all the better for enduring those long winters.

With all this statistical good news, one might wonder, what's Sweden's secret? First, it's important to note that statistics paint a broad picture, and even in the happiest places on Earth, there are individuals who are completely miserable. Nevertheless, Sweden seems to be doing something right.

By reputation, Swedes are generally quiet and reserved. Some outsiders say they are taciturn and depressed—even unfriendly. Some say dull; others say pessimistic. Swedes themselves admit to being shy, quiet, and boring. Is all this true? No, of course not; and well, maybe it is. Individuals, of course, have different personalities, and plenty of Swedes are jolly old souls, but the stereotypical Swedish character is most likely based on some kernel of truth. Anyone watching the movies of Sweden's most famous movie director and producer, Ingmar Bergman, could conclude that life in Sweden is lonely, meaningless, and depressing—albeit portrayed with artistic genius. Perhaps it's just another side effect of those long winters?

In truth, Swedes can be as warm and friendly as anyone. The culture reinforces a sense of practicality and moderation born of traditional Lutheran values. Extravagant excess, whether of material things, self-promotion, or emotionalism, are frowned on.

Observers of the Swedish way of life can point to other seeming paradoxes. Sweden is held up by fans and critics alike as a socialist or welfare state, and to some extent it is. The nation's official website calls it "capitalism done right"; after all, 95 percent of businesses are privately held. But Swedes pay some of the highest taxes in the world—up to 57 percent, depending on income levels, for individuals; 22 percent for corporations (in 2013).

In return the government provides for the greater welfare, which essentially eliminates poverty, subsidizes health care, child care, provides free education, and much more. Of course, the balance between government spending and balanced budgets can be a tricky point to achieve, and at times the equilibrium has gone off kilter. Swedish politicians debate these topics with each new election cycle. In recent years Sweden has had to make adjustments to its fiscal and social policies to maintain its economic stability, but for the most part, they have instituted successful reforms. Most Swedes believe they get their money's worth for the high taxes they pay, though naturally most wouldn't mind being able to keep more of their hard-earned kronor.

A modern building is part of the new Point Hyllie project in the southern city of Malmö.

Another factor shaking up Sweden's equilibrium is the influx of immigrants from parts of the world with very different cultures and traditions. In 2012, about 103,000 people moved to Sweden. The presence of immigrants in this country isn't new, but in the past, most newcomers came from other Scandinavian countries, the Baltic countries, and Northern Europe. Today, the new immigrants are coming in from North Africa, Western Asia, and

Investigators take pictures outside the Swedish bank Handelsbanken in Stockholm following a robbery attempt.

the Middle East. Sweden is committed to social equality, but the strains of cultural, religious, and language differences can't help but cause strife.

Immigrants represent about two hundred nationalities among Sweden's 9.7 million people. According to a study by the Swedish National Council for Crime Prevention in 1997–2001, 25 percent of the almost 1,520,000 crimes reported during that time were found to be committed by people born abroad. Another 20 percent were committed by Swedish-born people of foreign background. Were the immigrants more likely to commit crimes? Or were the Swedish law enforcement officials more likely to investigate people of foreign backgrounds? The study says immigrants were four times more likely to be investigated for lethal violence and robbery than were ethnic Swedes. Whatever the explanation, such findings indicate social problems.

Another conundrum is Sweden's high divorce rate. With all the benefits of Swedish life and family support, it seems contradictory that about half of Swedish marriages end in divorce. Marriage itself seems to be on the decline there, as it is in all the Scandinavian countries. While many observers might see these facts as indicative of problems inherent in the Swedish culture or society, some sociologists say they might signal something else. In a society which esteems and supports gender equality—especially the equal earning power of women—it may be that divorce and single parenthood simply are more viable alternatives than they were in the past, or still is in other cultures.

The increasingly secular nature of Sweden's society is likely also a factor. The changing attitudes and values regarding religion, marriage, and

The midnight sunlight shines on a lake in the northern part of Sweden.

family are part of a new Swedish reality. Time will tell where they take the society, but so far, indicators remain high that the country is working and working well.

On August 15, 2014, Sweden celebrated a landmark anniversary that few nations can claim: Two hundred years of peace. On that date in 1814, Sweden signed the peace agreement ending the brief Swedish-Norwegian War, Sweden's last war. Since that time, for two centuries, Sweden has not become involved militarily in any war.

Vikings and Volvos; Midsummer and the midnight sun; ABBA and Avicii; *Pippi Longstocking* and *The Girl with the Dragon Tattoo*; monarchy and democracy, socialism and capitalism—Sweden is a smorgasbord of contradictions and harmony, beloved traditions and progressive ideas, beautiful vistas and, for the most part, happy people.

GEOGRAPHY

A wooden windmill sits on the flat plains of Öland, an island off the coast of Småland in southern Sweden.

1

TO UNDERSTAND SWEDEN, IT HELPS to start with Scandinavia. Sweden is located on the Scandinavian Peninsula, a geographic landmass in northern Europe. The peninsula is made up of Norway on the west, Sweden on the east, and a part of Finland in the north. The peninsula is part of a broader region called Scandinavia, from which it gets its name. Scandinavia—the four countries of Norway, Sweden, Finland, and Denmark—is a region that shares a common heritage of culture, language, ethnicity, and language. Iceland is sometimes considered a part of Scandinavia, though geographically it is quite distant.

Although Scandinavia is part of Europe, its geographical position in the far north, separated from the rest of the continent by water, has historically kept it somewhat apart from Europe. Over the centuries, the region developed its own cultural characteristics. The seas that flow between the Scandinavian Peninsula and the Jutland Peninsula

Most people would not consider Sweden an island nation, but it has about 221,800 islands, mostly uninhabited, according to an official count in 2001. Of those, only 593 are larger than a square kilometer (about .386 sq mile). Buildings are on some 7,000 of the islands, but only 1,143 are considered inhabited.

The southeastern plains of Österlen are noted for their rural beauty.

of Denmark—the North Sea and the Baltic Sea—are no longer much of an obstacle, but Scandinavia remains a unique part of Europe.

Within Scandinavia, Sweden is its own unique place. It is a long, narrow country, extending 977 miles (1,572 kilometers) from north to south, and 310 miles (499 km) from west to east. It is the fifth largest country in Europe, with an area of 173,860 square miles (450,295 square km), making it only slightly larger than the U.S. state of California.

REGIONS

Sweden has a varied landscape of mountains, forests, rolling hills, lakes, and expansive plains. During the last ice age, about ten thousand years ago, massive glaciers sculpted mountains, lakes, and sandy ridges. They fertilized the soil of the central plains with finely ground material left behind as they retreated.

Sweden's northernmost province is called Lappland, a territory characterized by rolling hills, plains, and the highest mountains in Scandinavia. It also has forests of pine, spruce, and birch and a multitude of rivers and lakes. Its terrain crosses the Arctic Circle. Lappland's arctic climate allows for only a very short growing season; only a few crops, such as potatoes, grow here.

In medieval times, the region was thought to be an uninhabited "no man's land," but that assumption was wrong. People have lived in this cold part of the world since the Stone Age. It is the ancestral home of the Sami people, who came from the east about 4,000–5,000 years ago and still live here today. They inhabit a region called Sápmi (also known as Lapland, or the Laponian Area in English) that stretches across the northern portions of Norway, Sweden, Finland, and a small part of northwestern Russia.

In Swedish Lappland, there are still a few thousand Sami, but most people are descendants of settlers who came from other parts of the country to hunt for furs or work in the mines or forestry industries.

Reindeer run wild, or semi-wild, in this northern region. The nomadic Sami have long depended on reindeer for meat, fur, milk, and even transportation, though the old lifestyle is rapidly becoming outmoded. Some herders have adapted by running Christmas-themed businesses for tourists, who come to visit Father Christmas and ride on reindeer-pulled sleds.

A Sami reindeer herder and a traditional reindeer-skin tent.

The Kölen Mountains, which run from north to south, form the backbone of the Scandinavian Peninsula and act as a natural border between Sweden and Norway. Traditionally, Sweden is divided into three regions: Götaland, Svealand, and Norrland.

GÖTALAND The southernmost part of Sweden, called Götaland ("YUE-tah-land"), includes the county of Skåne, whose fertile plains are in fact a continuation of the flat lands of Denmark and northern Germany. The rest of Götaland is broken up by hills, lakes, and lowlands. The island of Öland, in the Baltic Sea, is also part of Götaland.

SVEALAND Svealand (SVEE-ah-land) refers to Sweden's central region, although it is actually in the southern part of the country. This region has hills, lowland plains, forests, and large river valleys. Sweden's capital, Stockholm, and second largest city, Göteborg (also called Gothenburg), are in Svealand. The island of Gotland, in the Baltic Sea, also forms part of Sweden's central region.

The rugged mountains of Kebnekaise National Park

NORRLAND Sweden's northern region, called Norrland (NOR-land), covers three-fifths of the country, yet it is only sparsely populated. Norrland is an important mining and forestry region. Sweden's oldest industrial region, Bergslagen, just north of Svealand, was founded on rich deposits of iron and other ores. Copper, lead, and zinc are mined in Västerbottencounty.

The country's highest peaks, Mount Kebnekaise at 6,926 feet (2,111 meters) and Mount Sarektjåkkå at 6,857 feet (2,090 m), are in Lappland, in the north of Norrland.

LAND OF THE MIDNIGHT SUN

Sweden has mild weather compared to other places on the same latitude (around sixty degrees north of the Equator), such as Alaska. Sweden's temperatures are moderated by the Gulf Stream and by warm westerly winds blowing in from the North Atlantic Ocean.

In July, the warmest month, average temperatures range from 14 degrees Celsius to 22 degrees Celsius (57 degrees Fahrenheit to 71 degrees Fahrenheit) in Stockholm and 12°C to 21°C (53°F to 69°F) in the northern city of Piteå.

Although winter temperatures vary considerably from north to south, Sweden generally experiences average temperatures below freezing in February, the coldest month, when average temperatures range from -5°C to -1°C (22°F to 30°F) in Stockholm and -14°C to -6°C (6°F to 22°F) in Piteå. In the south, snow covers the ground from December to March, while northern areas have snow cover from mid-October through mid-April.

In the summer, there is little difference in the weather between the north and south, as Norrland warms up as much as the south due to the long days.

The low sun creates days of continuous twilight during the winter in Lappland.

Sweden's arctic zone experiences about two months of continuous twilight in the winter and two months of continuous daylight in the summer. Long summer days and winter nights in this part of the world result from the tilt of the earth's axis as it rotates around the sun. Even in Stockholm, summer nights can be bright, with only a few hours of semi-darkness. This is why Sweden is called the Land of the Midnight Sun.

Overall the weather is milder in the southern coastal areas, which enjoy a longer fall and an earlier spring. Spring may arrive in the southern county of Skåne in February, while the northern region of Lappland may only see the end of winter in late May.

FLORA AND FAUNA

Forests cover about 68 percent of Sweden's land area; most are found in the northern, temperate coniferous belt. Spruce and pines are common, although linden, ash, maple, birch, and aspen are also found. Flowering plants, such as orchids and rock roses, are found in parts of the mountain range and on the islands of Gotland and Öland.

A Scandinavian landscape in summer.

THE ÖRESUND BRIDGE

Seven thousand years ago, the lands that make up Sweden and Denmark were connected, but rising sea levels eventually came between them. In 1991, the governments of the two countries agreed to build a bridge across the Öresund Strait to reconnect not only Sweden and Denmark, but

The Öresund bridge between Denmark and Sweden, as seen from Malmö.

the Scandinavian Peninsula and mainland Europe. The bridge opened in 2000 and now carries about 17,000 vehicles a day.

The Öresund Bridge, or Öresundsbron in Swedish, is more than just a bridge. It is a 4.9-mile (7.8-km) bridge for both automotive and rail traffic from Skane, Sweden, to a 2.5-mile (4-km) long artificial island, named Peberholm, where it becomes a road which then descends under the sea into a 2.5-mile (4-km) tunnel which emerges on the island of Zealand in Denmark. (Or the reverse—from tunnel to island to bridge—if traveling from Denmark to Sweden.) The total span is just over 10 miles (16.4 km), which makes it the longest combined road and rail bridge in Europe.

The bridge complex was built this way to provide a clear channel for ships over the tunnel portion, and to avoid interfering with air traffic from the nearby Copenhagen International Airport.

Lemmings, which resemble guinea pigs, are common critters in Sweden.

Animal life has been affected by climate changes since the last ice age and also by human settlement. Bears and lynx roam the northern forests, while large numbers of roe deer, moose, hare, and fox are found throughout the country. Motorists often have to stop for moose crossing roads in the forest.

In the winter, many birds leave Sweden for warmer places, while in the summer, migratory birds fly in from as far away as Egypt and southern Africa. Bird lovers in the countryside have a chance to spot species such as the rare white-tailed eagle, the wild swan, and the redshank.

Sweden is also home to furry, brown rodents called lemmings. A common myth about lemmings is that every few years, they go through a cycle of mass suicides—they migrate in groups to the coast, where they jump into the sea and drown. Scientists say it's not true. Nevertheless, lemming population numbers do rise and fall in response to a number of factors. In Sweden, a year when the numbers are high is called "a lemming year."

Sweden's long coastline and many lakes are home to a rich variety of aquatic life. Fish include cod and mackerel from the salty Atlantic and salmon and pike from the less saline waters of the Gulf of Bothnia and the lakes and rivers. Traditional food staples include herring such as the *strömming* (STROHM-ming) species from the Baltic.

To protect the animals, hunting and fishing are strictly regulated. The government has set aside twenty areas of natural beauty for preservation as national parks. Sweden was the first nation in Europe to establish national parks in 1910. The largest and most famous park in Sweden is Sareks National Park in the Lappland region.

A man fishes from a small boat.

THE MILDER SOUTH

More than 85 percent of Sweden's 9.7 million people live in the south, which has fertile land and a mild climate. The most densely populated areas are within the triangle formed by the three largest urban centers of Stockholm, Göteborg, and Malmö. These cities hold about a third of Sweden's population. Fewer people live in the north. On average, Norrland has only six persons per square mile (two persons per square km).

STOCKHOLM Stockholm is not only surrounded by water, it is made up of fourteen islands and portions of the mainland. The city islands are part of the greater Stockholm archipelago, a group of some 30,000 islands off the east coast of Sweden. The city itself spreads across the easternmost part of the freshwater Lake Mälaren, where the lake meets the Baltic Sea. The fresh and salt waters are separated by the island of the old city, Gamla Stan, and great artificial canals at the southern end.

Stockholm is also Sweden's most important commercial center; more than one-quarter of the labor force works in Greater Stockholm. There are some 902,000 people living in Stockholm—close to 2.2 million in the greater metropolitan area—but the urban area spreads over 2,500 square miles (6,519 sq. km), so it is not crowded. Reflecting typical Swedish concern for the environment, the waters around the city are kept clean and are filled with fish. It is common to see anglers fishing for their dinner right in the heart of the city. In the summer it is popular for leisure activities, with many summer homes on the islands.

GÖTEBORG (YEH-TA-BORY) With 536,800 inhabitants, Göteborg (also known as Gothenburg in English) is the country's second largest city and its most important port, located on the western coast. It is also an important industrial center for Sweden's aerospace, automotive, and other engineering industries.

MALMÖ (MAHL-MUH) With a population of 303,900, Malmö is an important port on the southern tip of Sweden. The *Öresund Bridge* connects Malmö to Copenhagen, Denmark, across the Öresund Strait. Among the local industries are shipbuilding and automotive production. Located in Sweden's most fertile agricultural region, Malmö also exports agricultural products.

The Turning Torso skyscraper in Malmö, which opened in 2005, is the tallest building in Scandinavia. It rises 623 feet (190 meters).

INTERNET LINKS

international.stockholm.se
"City of Stockholm" is an attractive, user-friendly site with news, information, and photos of the various attractions in the city.

sweden.se/nature/preserving-nature-in-sweden
"Preserving Nature in Sweden" is part of the official website Sweden.se.

travel.nationalgeographic.com/travel/countries/sweden-guide
National Geographic travel guide to Sweden offers facts, map, and photos.

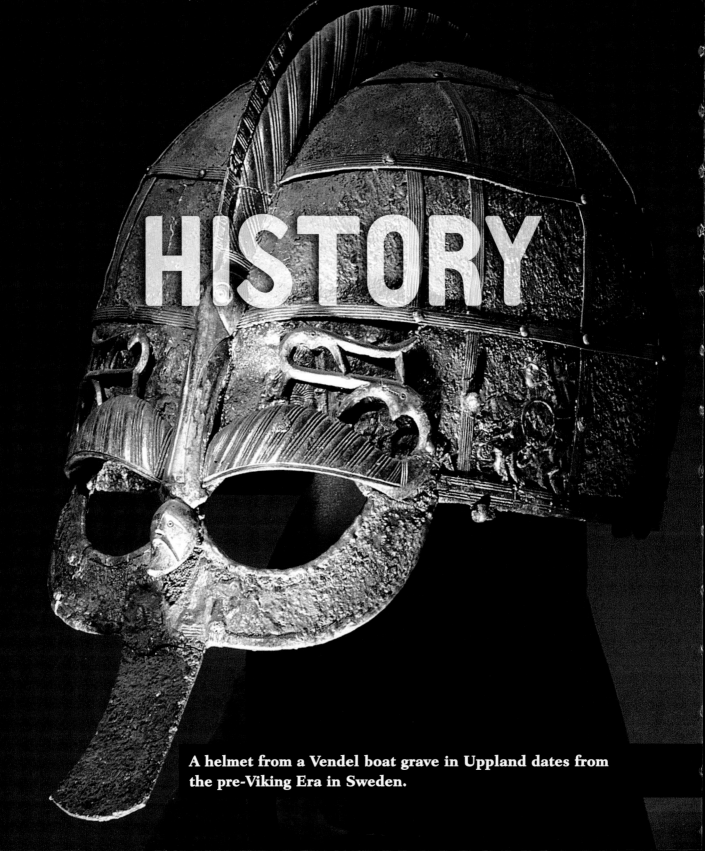

HISTORY

A helmet from a Vendel boat grave in Uppland dates from the pre-Viking Era in Sweden.

2

FOURTEEN THOUSAND YEARS AGO, no people lived in the land that would become Sweden. It was covered by thick glacial ice. But over time, the ice began to recede and it didn't take long for Stone Age hunters and gatherers to move in. The first signs of human habitation in Sweden date to about 12,000 years ago, but around 8000 to 6000 BCE, greater numbers of nomadic people started to populate the area, leaving simple stone tools behind.

EARLIEST PEOPLE

Archaeologists have uncovered bronze weapons and religious artifacts from the Bronze Age, around 1800 to 500 BCE, that indicate a high level of culture.

The development of such a society continued over the period of the great migrations from 400 to 500 CE and over the Vendel period from 550 to 800 CE. The Vendel period is named for the discovery of splendid boat graves at Vendel in the region of Uppland, where the Svea tribe settled. It is from this tribe that the name *Sverige* or Sweden originated. In the sixth century, the warring Sveas began to exert their influence

Queen Kristina, who reigned from 1632 to 1654, is the only female monarch of the modern Swedish kingdom. She took the throne in 1632, just before her sixth birthday, although she was not officially crowned until 1644, when she turned eighteen. But in 1654, Kristina abdicated, converted to Catholicism, and settled in Rome.

over their neighbors. A series of minor wars occurred, and by the beginning of the Viking Era in 800 CE, the Sveas had expanded beyond their original seat of power at Lake Mälaren.

THE VIKINGS

The Viking Era lasted only a short time, from 800 to 1050 CE. In that time, these sea-faring people left a strong impression on history. The name Viking comes from an old word *vik* (vick), meaning "bay or creek," places where the Vikings kept their famous longships. The Vikings were excellent sailors, skilled in shipbuilding. Their longships were strong enough to sail in stormy seas, and the boats' round-bottomed hulls allowed them to beach for surprise attacks.

The Vikings sailed from their home bases in Sweden, Norway, and Denmark in their longships, attacking other countries across northern Europe. The first recorded Viking raid took place in the late eighth century. It was an attack on a rich abbey at Lindisfarne on the northeastern coast of England.

A replica of a Viking longship sails on the Baltic Sea.

As a result, people described Vikings as barbarians who killed monks and burned books. The Vikings were fierce warriors who showed their enemies no mercy, and they acquired such a ferocious reputation that in many parts of Europe, people prayed, "From the fury of the Norsemen, Good Lord deliver us." Viking warriors showed little fear in battle. They believed that if they died in battle, their souls would go to Valhalla, their equivalent of heaven.

Like the Vikings themselves, the old Norse mythology has also left its mark. The gods Odin (god of wisdom), Thor (god of thunder), Frey (god of fertility), and a pantheon of others are well known today.

The Vikings were known not only for plundering but also for trade and expansionism. Vikings from Sweden swept east along the Baltic coast and down along rivers leading to Russia. They set up trading stations and principalities in Russia, like that of the grand prince Rurik at Novgorod. They also went as far as the Black and Caspian seas, where they formed trade links with the Byzantine Empire and the Arab states. Some of these Vikings even remained in Byzantium (Constantinople) as members of an elite imperial guard.

Around the tenth century, Vikings from Sweden founded the city of Kiev in Russia as a result of profitable trade in furs, honey, and amber. These travelers also took home gold and silver, and luxury goods such as cloth. These goods, as well as artifacts such as coins from Arabia, have been found at the site of Sweden's first city, Birka, on the island of Björkö on Lake Mälaren. This fertile island was the first center of power in Sweden. Today, the nation's capital also lies partially on this important lake.

EARLY CHRISTIANITY

The Vikings' expeditions caused Europeans to become aware of the Scandinavian lands in the north. In the ninth century, Ansgar, a Benedictine monk born in France, arrived in Sweden to introduce Christianity.

He succeeded in converting some of the inhabitants, but it would take two more centuries for Christianity to overcome indigenous Viking religious beliefs. By the mid-twelfth century, when King Erik Jedvarsson converted to Christianity, paganism was no longer practiced and Sweden became a Christian country. King Erik was later canonized as Saint Erik and became the patron saint of Sweden.

A statue of Saint Erik the Holy (King Erik) adorns Uppsala Cathedral.

A statue of Birger Jarl, founder of Stockholm, stands in the Gamla Stan (Old Town) section of the city.

UNITING A KINGDOM

Although Sweden became unified in 1000 CE, the monarchy was still not the central authority. Each province had its own assembly and laws.

After 1250 a new family dynasty called Folkung ruled Sweden. The Folkung was more successful in controlling the provinces. Its first administrator was Birger Jarl, who founded Stockholm and at the same time issued national laws.

In 1280 his son Magnus Ladulås introduced a form of feudalism, which is a social and economic system in which the nobility own vast tracts of land and peasants living on the land are obliged to provide the lord with labor and a share of their crops. A council of nobles and church officials was established to advise the king. The farmers, however, held on to their ancient rights and prevented the implementation of a full feudal system. These ancient rights, which had been handed down orally and were first put into written form in this period, formed Europe's oldest body of written law. By the mid-fourteenth century, a code of law for the whole country was established during the reign of King Magnus Eriksson.

THE HANSEATIC PERIOD

In the fourteenth century, trade in the Baltic region flourished under the leadership of the Hanseatic League, an association of German towns. Sweden also benefited from trade with the Hanseatic League, and the town of Visby on the island of Gotland became an important trading post.

Sweden's economy prospered, and many new towns were founded. German influence spread to the political, social, and cultural spheres. The language assimilated many linguistic forms from the German spoken by the

Hanseatic traders. However, in spite of enhanced trading activity, agriculture remained the basis of the economy and developed through improved methods and tools.

In the mid-fourteenth century, a plague called "The Black Death" swept Europe and did not spare Sweden—one-third of the people died. Sweden's economy collapsed, as many farms were abandoned. It only recovered in the second half of the fifteenth century, when iron production played a more important role in the economy.

UNION WITH DENMARK

In 1389, the Swedish royal council elected Queen Margrethe of Denmark as ruler of Sweden. Margrethe was an intelligent, astute queen. In 1397 a treaty called the Union of Kalmar united Denmark, Norway, and Sweden under the rule of one crown. However, after Margrethe's death, there were conflicts between the monarchy, the nobility, and Sweden's heavily taxed farmers.

Conflicts between the Danes and Swedes eventually led to the "Bloodbath of Stockholm" in 1520, when Denmark's King Kristian II invaded Sweden and

Soon after the Stockholm Bloodbath, Gustav Vasa had a series of images made to commemorate the carnage. In this one, an executioner at left prepares to decapitate a bishop while, at right, soldiers drag off the already decapitated heads and bodies.

Kalmar Castle, home of the Vasa kings, is reflected in the harbor.

executed eighty-two leading noblemen. This terrible act spurred a rebellion and the downfall of Kristian II. The leader of the rebellion, Swedish nobleman Gustav Vasa, whose father and other relatives were killed in the Bloodbath, was crowned king of Sweden in 1523.

GUSTAV VASA

Sometimes called "the George Washington of Sweden," King Gustav Vasa established the foundation for Sweden's statehood. The Swedes consider him the founder of their nation; June 6, the day he was crowned king in 1523, is today celebrated as Sweden's National Day.

During his reign, which lasted until 1560, Gustav Vasa made many important changes to the administration of the country. He made Stockholm the capital of Sweden and, to gain greater political control, seized the property of the Roman Catholic Church. He encouraged the spread of Protestantism and laid the ground for Lutheranism as Sweden's state religion. In 1527 a national assembly, or parliament, was created with representatives of the four estates, or social classes—nobles, clergymen, burghers, and peasants.

In 1544, Vasa declared a hereditary monarchy in Sweden. Previously, the king was elected, which meant that each time the throne was vacant, the

Swedish nobility fought for power. In providing for a hereditary monarchy, Gustav Vasa became the founder of the Vasa dynasty that would rule Sweden for the next three hundred years.

SWEDISH EXPANSION

After Gustav Vasa's death, his sons struggled for the throne. From 1560 to 1611, the crown passed between three of his sons. But in spite of the infighting, Sweden prospered. The University of Uppsala, founded in 1477, flourished. Immigration was encouraged.

Sweden's next great king was Gustavus II Adolphus, grandson of Gustav Vasa. During his rule from 1611 to 1632, the kingdom expanded to include part of the Baltic region and Poland. Gustavus II also drove the Danes out of southern Sweden and made his country more powerful than Denmark for the first time.

In 1654, Karl X Gustav took the throne and maintained Sweden's expansionist policy. Under his reign, Sweden reached the height of its

Uppsala University is the oldest university in Sweden, founded in 1477.

Gustav III ruled
Sweden during
the time of the
American and
French revolutions.

geographical size and political importance. It won Skåne province from Denmark, and after 1658, Sweden became a great power in northern Europe. The kingdom included Finland, provinces in northern Germany, and the Baltic state that is now Estonia. For a while, there was even a Swedish colony on the Delaware River in North America.

During his rule from 1696 to 1718, the next king, Karl XI, lost much of Sweden's Baltic empire and parts of Finland to Russia. Karl XII's defeat in the twenty-one-year Great Northern War against Denmark, Poland, and Russia reduced the country's borders to largely those of Sweden and Finland today.

SCIENCE AND CULTURE

The eighteenth century was an era of cultural and scientific growth. Parliament passed a Freedom of the Press Act in 1766, making Sweden one of the first countries in the world to protect press freedom. This act is still in force today. Many Swedes made important scientific contributions to the world: Carl von Linné, also called Linnaeus, created a system of classifying plants and animals that is used worldwide today; Anders Celsius invented the centigrade thermometer; Emmanuel Swedenborg made important discoveries in metallurgy, but is most well-known for his religious writings.

Gustavus III (reigned 1771—1792) encouraged the development of the fine arts. He was responsible for the building of the Stockholm Dramatic Theater and the magnificent Royal Opera House. He also founded several academies for the fine arts, most notably the Swedish Academy of Literature, which is well known today for awarding the Nobel Prize for Literature.

Gustavus III sealed his fate, however, when he dissolved the parliament and tried to seize absolute power. He also became politically involved in a plot to reinstate the French king Louis XVI to the throne during the French Revolution. By this time, he had many enemies and in 1792 he was shot in

ALFRED NOBEL AND THE NOBEL PRIZE

Internationally, one of the best known Swedes in history is Alfred Nobel. Born in Stockholm, he grew up in St. Petersburg, Russia, where his father worked as a weapons manufacturer. Alfred developed an interest in literature, philosophy, and chemistry, and spoke five languages fluently by the time he was seventeen.

As an adult, back in Stockholm, he devoted himself to the study of explosives, to help the family business. Nobel was a chemist, an inventor, engineer, and author, but he is best remembered for his invention of dynamite in 1867. Dynamite was safer than other explosives used at the time, and proved invaluable in the mining and construction industries.

Despite his work producing armaments, Nobel was a pacifist. He didn't want to be remembered as a "merchant of death" as some newspapers had dubbed him. After his death, he left his wealth in trust to establish the foundation that would award the Nobel Prize.

Today, these prizes are awarded annually in three branches of science—physics, chemistry, and medical science—as well as in literature, and a related award in economics. The ultimate award is the Peace Prize, given to the individual or group who best advances the cause of world peace. Some of the people who have won the Nobel Peace Prize include Martin Luther King, Jr., in 1964; Mother Theresa in 1979; and Nelson Mandela in 1993.

the back during a midnight masquerade ball at the Royal Opera House in Stockholm. He died thirteen days later.

NEW DYNASTY

During the Napoleonic Wars in the early nineteenth century, Sweden lost more of its territories—Finland to Russia and the German provinces to France—and faced an economic crisis. There was widespread unhappiness under the rule of Gustavus IV Adolphus, and he was deposed. His uncle, Karl XIII, was elected as the next king.

Parliamentary rule was again introduced. As Karl XIII had no heir, the parliament elected Jean-Baptiste Bernadotte, a French marshal close to Napoleon Bonaparte, to be heir to the throne in 1810. After the Napoleonic Wars in 1814, Bernadotte obtained large compensation for the loss of Sweden's Finnish lands and forced Norway to give in to Swedish rule. His conservative policies won him the support of the old ruling class, but a liberal opposition began to form.

The reigns of his son and grandson, Oscar I and Karl XV, saw liberal ideas become reality. These included the setting up of compulsory education and elementary schools, and the implementation of free trade. In the latter half of the nineteenth century, rail transportation enabled the development of forest industries. But Sweden remained poor, with 90 percent of its people dependent on agriculture. Many emigrated, mainly to North America, between 1866 and 1914. More than one million Swedes, or about one-fifth of the population, left for greener pastures.

THE TWENTIETH CENTURY AND BEYOND

The twentieth century saw Sweden transform into a modern industrial state. Universal suffrage was introduced for men in 1909 and for women in 1919. Sweden was among the first countries to give women the right to vote.

In 1905 Norway gained full independence from Sweden, and the two countries have remained good neighbors, more or less, ever since.

TWO WORLD WARS During World War I (1914—1918) and World War II (1939—1945), Sweden remained neutral. As a result, it was a safe haven for many refugees fleeing Nazi occupation in Europe during WWII. On the other hand, during that same war, Sweden allowed German troops to march through the country on their way to occupy Norway, and also exported iron ore to Nazi Germany, which called Swedish neutrality into question.

Sweden was never attacked or occupied by Germany. The reasons are complicated, but essentially, Hitler saw it in Germany's best interest to leave Sweden alone. It was dependent upon Swedish metal ore from the mines in the northern part of the country. For Sweden's part, it was willing to cooperate to some extent with Germany in return for being left out of the hostilities.

SOCIAL WELFARE STATE In 1932, during a time of worldwide economic downturn and high unemployment, the Social Democrats created a new

Allied prisoners of war (POWs) arrive at the train station in Trelleborg, Sweden, in 1944. During World War II, the Swedish Red Cross brokered a series of POW exchanges between the Germans and the Allies.

A model demonstrates a Swedish-made seat belt in 1957.

policy. The Swedish government would provide the unemployed with meaningful jobs, which would in turn vitalize the economy and create more new jobs. This would, however, require heavily increased taxes, and with the advent of two World Wars, would have to wait.

When World War II came to an end, Sweden emerged in a very strong position. Europe was devastated, but Swedish industry was intact and ready to manufacture products that Europe desperately needed. This caused an economic boom in Sweden, which helped to finance the further development of the Swedish welfare state (the *folkhemmet*) during the 1950s and 1960s. Swedes saw their standard of living rise quickly, and poverty was virtually eliminated.

HARD TIMES As the twentieth century came to a close, a number of things went sour in Sweden. In 1986, Prime Minister Olof Palme was assassinated as he and his wife walked home from a cinema in Stockholm. That the prime minister could walk the streets without bodyguards is a commentary on Swedish life at the time. The murder and bungled police investigation shocked not only Swedes, but the world. The crime remains unsolved, though numerous theories abound. In 2014, hints pointing to the possible motive and murderer arose once again in the media, as they have from time to time.

In the 1990s, against the background of a worldwide recession, Sweden suffered an economic downturn that some blamed on the burdens of the welfare state. The Swedish currency was devalued and interest rates, taxes, inflation, and unemployment figures shot up rapidly. It was in this climate that Swedes voted to join the European Union in 1995. However, the Swedes never joined most of Europe in making the Euro its currency. The government instituted major reforms and the economy improved. During the subsequent world economic crisis of 2008, Sweden weathered the storm exceptionally well due to lessons learned in the 1990s.

In 2003, Sweden suffered another shock when Foreign Minister Anna Lindh was stabbed to death while shopping in a department store in Stockholm (without bodyguards). This time, the crime was solved; the assailant was determined to be mentally ill, and the killing is not considered a political assassination.

"Do you want the krona or the euro?" is written on a tent in Stockholm in 2003, as Swedes debate the issue prior to a nationwide referendum.

INTERNET LINKS

www.bbc.com/news/world-europe-17961621
BBC's timeline of key events in Sweden since 1095.

www.nobelprize.org
The official site of the Nobel Prize has a wealth of information about Alfred Nobel and the many laureates who have won the awards.

sweden.se/society/history-of-sweden
"History of Sweden" on the official Sweden.se website is a good overview.

GOVERNMENT

Swedish flags wave in an open field.

3

THE KINGDOM OF SWEDEN IS A constitutional monarchy. The king (or queen) is the head of the country, but the nation's constitution defines and guides the government.

The main principal of Swedish government is that all power flows from the people. Every citizen has a say, has the same rights, and the same opportunity to have a voice. The Parliament is the foremost representative of the people. Everyone is free to criticize politicians and public agencies. If people don't like their representatives, they have a chance every four years to vote in someone new.

The Parliament House, the seat of the Riksdag, is located on an island in Stockholm.

The design of Sweden's flag follows that of Denmark's flag, while the colors—blue and yellow—are from the Swedish coat of arms. June 6, Sweden's National Day, was originally celebrated as Swedish Flag Day. This was the day on which Gustav Vasa, founder of the Swedish state, was elected king in 1523. It was also on this day in 1809 that the country adopted a new constitution enshrining civil rights and liberties.

THE CONSTITUTION

The Swedish constitution, consisting of three documents, defines the principles of government and describes the rights and freedoms of the people. The most important document in the constitution is the Instrument of Government, which states the basic rules of government and society. The most recent version was adopted in 1975 and last amended in 2011. It states that all public power comes from the people and that democracy is based on "freedom of opinion and on universal and equal suffrage."

There are different types of rights and freedoms, and the Instrument of Government defines them. Absolute rights, which cannot be restricted except through a constitutional amendment, include freedom of worship; protection from being forced to declare political and religious views; protection of citizenship; and the prohibition against capital punishment, or death sentence. Rights that may be restricted by the law are freedom of speech, freedom of association, and protection from the restraint of liberty. The constitution also covers how far these restrictions may extend.

Sweden has had a king for more a thousand years—its monarchy is one of the oldest in the world. The king is the head of state and performs official duties, such as opening the new session of Parliament every October. He has no political power and no role in politics. King Carl XVI Gustaf, a descendant of the Bernadotte family, came to the throne in 1973. He acts as the official representative of Sweden. His wife, or consort, is Queen Silvia.

Carl XVI will be succeeded by his daughter, Crown Princess Victoria, the eldest of his three children, born in July 1977. The heir to the throne is traditionally the firstborn, and in 1979 the Act of Succession was amended to give men and women equal rights to the throne. (Previously, sons took precedence over daughters.) The king's and queen's two other children are Prince Carl Philip, born in 1979, and Princess Madeleine, born in 1982.

Sweden's royal family used to live in the Royal Palace in Stockholm, the largest of Sweden's royal palaces. (Today this huge building houses three museums.) However, since 1981, they have lived in the Drottningholm Palace, shown here, a UNESCO World Heritage site, on an island on the outskirts of Stockholm.

The second constitutional document is the Act of Succession, which regulates the succession to the throne. The third document, the Freedom of the Press Act, provides the right to publish without restrictions and allows citizens access to all public papers. Sweden was the first country in the world to introduce freedom of the press in 1766.

CHIEF OF STATE King Carl XVI Gustaf has been the chief of state since September 19, 1973. The heir apparent to the throne is Princess Victoria, the daughter of the king. If she succeeds her father to the throne as expected, she will be Sweden's fourth queen regnant—that is, queen in her own right as opposed to being a queen consort, the wife of a king—and the first such queen since 1720.

HEAD OF GOVERNMENT Prime minister Fredrik Reinfeldt of the Moderate Party held this office from 2006 to 2014, having been reelected in 2010. The deputy prime minister, Jan Bjorklund, of the Liberal People's Party, assumed office in 2010, forming a coalition government with Reinfeldt. They were defeated in the 2014 general election by the social Democrats.

PARLIAMENT

Sweden's unicameral (one-chamber) parliament, or Riksdag ("RICKS-dahg"), has 349 members. They are elected by popular vote on a proportional representation basis and serve four-year terms. It is the main representative of the people. Swedes age eighteen and above have the right to vote, and voter turnout is usually high, at more than 80 percent, although voting is not compulsory. The functions of Parliament are to make laws, decide on taxes, and determine the state budget. The parliament has a great influence on foreign policy.

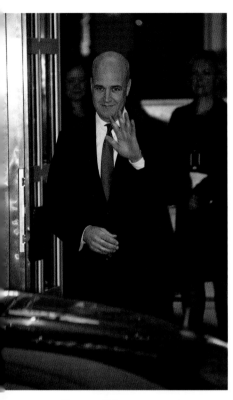

Former Prime Minister Fredrik Reinfeldt waves during an official occasion in Stockholm.

EXECUTIVE POWER

Political power lies with the cabinet and the party or parties to which ministers belong. The cabinet is made up of the prime minister and twenty-one ministers, who have to give up their right to vote in parliament if they join the cabinet; official substitutes take their places. Cabinet ministers are appointed by the prime minister.

POLITICAL PARTIES

After World War I, voting rights were expanded and political parties began to gain prominence. In the 1921 election, five parties were voted into parliament: the Social Democrats, the Communists, the Moderates, the Liberals, and the Centrists. The Social Democrats soon became the dominant party.

The socialist government introduced a mixed economy, where both the public and private sectors played important roles in economic development. Known as "the middle way," this form of government soon gained Sweden a reputation for industrial progress and political stability. For many decades, the Social Democratic Party had a dominant role in Swedish politics. However, over the past thirty years, power has changed hands several times between the Social Democrats and the "non-socialist" political bloc.

Here is a quick description of the today's major parties:

A woman walks past election posters advertising different political parties for the European elections in Stockholm on May 25, 2014.

THE SOCIAL DEMOCRATIC PARTY has a base of blue-collar workers, public sector employees, and trade unions. It is committed to social welfare programs and government direction of the economy.

THE MODERATE PARTY emphasizes personal freedom and free enterprise while still supporting social benefits. Its voter base is urban business people and professionals, young voters, and some blue-collar workers.

THE GREEN PARTY is a left-leaning, environmentalist party that attracts young people, particularly in the big cities. It strongly supports replacing nuclear energy in Sweden with alternative energy sources.

THE LIBERAL PARTY supports "social responsibility without socialism," favoring the European Union and a free-market economy combined with social welfare programs. Foreign aid, education, and women's equality also are popular issues. Its voter base is mainly the educated middle class.

THE CENTER PARTY is popular in rural Sweden. It supports a healthy economic climate for business and job creation, rural development, as well as climate change and environmental concerns.

THE SWEDEN DEMOCRATS won representation in Parliament for the first time in 2010. It is a nationalist, right-wing party. It seeks to protect Swedish culture and values, mostly by reducing the flow of immigrants into the country. The party finds support among the unemployed, laborers, men, and people in their twenties.

THE LEFT PARTY, formerly the Communist Party, focuses on feminist issues, public sector power, and the environment. It opposes privatization and Swedish participation in NATO activities. Its base is made up of some young people, government employees, feminists, journalists, and former social democrats.

THE CHRISTIAN DEMOCRATIC PARTY is concerned with conservative social values. It finds support among members of conservative churches and rural populations. Christian Democrats seek government support for families and a focus on ethical practices.

LOCAL GOVERNMENT

The clocktower of the Malmö City Hall.

The Swedish administration is divided into twenty-one counties consisting of 288 municipalities in total. Each county is run by an elected council headed by a governor appointed at the federal level. Each municipality is also run by an elected council.

The county council is chiefly responsible for providing medical care and training nurses and other health care professionals. Besides a few government-run and private hospitals, the county councils own all hospitals in Sweden. County councils also see to the development of educational facilities, the proper functioning of social services, public transportation, industry, and tourism within the county.

Municipal councils have a lot of decision-making power in matters affecting residents within the municipality, such as child and elderly care, education in elementary, intermediate, and high school, taxes and service fees, garbage collection and disposal, and the supply of electricity and gas.

To fulfill their responsibilities, both county and municipal councils are entitled to levy taxes. They also receive federal subsidies.

THE OMBUDSMAN

The ombudsman is a Swedish concept, created to provide some kind of check on the work of public agencies. Besides monitoring these agencies, the ombudsman also looks into complaints from the public against unfair treatment. This idea has spread to other countries and institutions with the aim of protecting the individual.

Lars Augustin Mannerheim, a nobleman and politician, was the first Swedish parliamentary ombudsman.

The oldest form of ombudsmanship is the office of the parliamentary ombudsman that dates from 1809. It was created to give the parliament a safeguard for how laws were used by judges, civil servants, and military officers. Today there are four parliamentary ombudsmen who cover all national and municipal agencies in Sweden. These ombudsmen investigate thousands of complaints annually, choosing either to mediate or to take legal action against the offending party.

Other government-appointed ombudsmen include the competition ombudsman, whose job is to ensure fair business practices based on the law, and the consumer ombudsman, whose work is to protect consumer rights. The consumer ombudsman tries to ensure that consumers are protected

SWEDEN'S NEUTRALITY POLICY

During World Wars I and II, Sweden managed to keep its neutrality thanks to a combination of political will, diplomatic skill, and just plain luck. After all, during WWII, both Norway and Denmark—also neutral—were occupied by the Germans, but Sweden was not.

After World War II, Sweden needed to decide whether to remain neutral or join the North Atlantic Treaty Organization (NATO) along with Norway and Denmark. Joining would mean aligning itself with the other NATO countries (which includes much of Europe, as well as Canada and the United States) for purposes of mutual defense in wartime, and would invalidate its neutrality.

Ultimately Sweden declined to join NATO, and stuck with a policy of keeping neutrality as an option if the country so decided. The purpose was to keep Sweden out of any alliance in peacetime, therefore enabling neutrality in a war situation.

However, in 1995, Sweden joined the European Union, an economic alliance which officially ended its neutrality policy. Nevertheless, Sweden remains militarily non-aligned, a status that allows it to cooperate with NATO through the framework of Partnership for Peace (PfP). (PfP is a NATO program aimed at creating trust between NATO and other nonmember states in Europe and the former Soviet Union.) Sweden's current position is that it will choose the scope of its involvement based on Sweden's interest as a country that is not part of a military alliance.

NATO Secretary General Anders Fogh Rasmussen and then-Swedish Prime Minister Fredrik Reinfeldt speak during a press conference at the government headquarters in Stockholm.

against misleading advertising, unsafe products, and improper business practices such as unreasonable contracts.

The press ombudsman is not appointed by the government but has been established by three national press organizations. The press ombudsman examines complaints by people who think that certain newspaper stories have violated press ethics and wish to be protected against the invasion of their privacy. There are also ombudsmen who work against ethnic discrimination and unfair treatment based on sexual orientation, and ombudsmen who work for equality for the disabled.

INTERNET LINKS

sweden.se/society/the-swedish-system-of-government
The Swedish System of Government, as described on the official website of Sweden.

www.riksdagen.se
Official website of the Riksdag; click to translate into English.

www.kungahuset.se
The website of the Swedish Royal Court translates nicely into English with a click, and has news and information on the members of the royal family and the royal palaces.

www.government.se/sb/d/11725/a/122836
"Sweden and NATO" is a clarification of Sweden's position, as posted on the Swedish government website.

ECONOMY

A man communicates using Skype, a company based in Sweden.

4

SWEDEN IS A HIGHLY INDUSTRIALIZED country, with one of the world's leading economies and highest living standards. It has a competitive mixed economy, in which private and state-owned enterprises exist side by side. About 90 percent of all companies and resources are privately owned; 5 percent are state owned and 5 percent are owned as cooperatives. This "Swedish model" refers to the way Sweden fostered prosperity by avoiding the pitfalls of both communism and capitalism.

THE SWEDISH MODEL

Since 1932 Sweden's socialist government has steered "the middle way" by allowing the private and public sectors to develop together. This was very successful for many years. A key factor was the cooperation of the three main players in the economy: government, labor, and business. Unlike in other socialist nations, the government in Sweden did not nationalize key industries.

During World War II, Sweden declared neutrality and therefore didn't have to rebuild its economy in the wake of the war the way other European countries did. This gave it an advantage, allowing for a high

Swedish carmaker Saab was the first to include seatbelts as standard equipment in 1958. The three-point seatbelt, one of the most important car safety innovations of all time, was invented in 1959 by Nils Bohlin for Volvo. Today it is standard in every passenger vehicle, and is estimated to have saved a life every six minutes since its launch.

Bana 1:2

At a Volvo plant in Torslanda, car chassis move along on the production line during the early stages of assembly.

standard of living for its population in the second half of the twentieth century. Today, a mere 1 percent of its population is considered to be living in poverty. For comparison, 15 percent of Americans live in poverty. Swedes have achieved a literacy rate of 99 percent and live, on average, five years longer than Americans. Naturally, the comparative statistics represent many very complicated factors, but they are still worth noting.

MAJOR INDUSTRIAL SECTORS

Sweden has an export-oriented economy. Its labor force is skilled and highly educated. Modern Swedish companies make specialized products, use high technology, and emphasize research and development. More than 40 percent of the industrial labor force is employed by the country's twenty largest companies. Some well-known Swedish companies include Electrolux appliances, Ericsson cell phones, H&M attire, IKEA home furnishings, AstraZeneca pharmaceuticals, Spotify online music service, and Skype voice and video software app.

ENGINEERING This is the largest sector of the economy, accounting for about 50 percent of industrial production and concentrated in southern and central Sweden, especially in the urban areas of Stockholm, Göteborg, and Malmö.

The engineering sector includes mechanical engineering, electrical engineering, the manufacture of transportation equipment, and metal fabrication. The most important is the automotive industry, which exports 70 percent of its output. The major auto manufacturer, Volvo, is a producer of cars, trucks, buses, and heavy engines.

Electrical engineering and electronics form another vital sector. Products include telecommunications systems, computers, and industrial robots. Telecommunications equipment accounts for 40 percent of electrical production. The ratio of robots to workers in Sweden is among the highest in the world.

CONSTRUCTION Little new housing has been built in Sweden in the last twenty years. This has led to a housing shortage. The Swedish government is making housing policy a priority in an effort to stimulate new construction.

Internationally, Swedish construction companies have done well, helping to build infrastructural projects such as dams, harbors, railways, and power stations in many countries. The chief advantage of these companies lies in technical knowledge and project management. Their largest export markets are Middle Eastern and African countries. Export construction projects are a vital factor in the long-term growth of Sweden's construction industry, which employs almost 20 percent of the total labor force.

IRON AND STEEL Today the production of engineered products flourishes as a result of the domestic manufacture of iron and nonferrous metal goods.

Although mining has now declined in importance, Sweden remains the largest iron ore exporter in Europe. About 90 percent of Sweden's iron comes from the great ore fields at Kiruna and Malmberget in the Lappland region. Copper, lead, zinc, silver, and gold are also mined in large amounts in the north.

Sweden's two most iconic automotive brands are Volvo and Saab. Both have loyal customers outside Sweden, including the United States, where their share of the auto market is small but passionate. However, unlike Volvo, Saab's export market was limited to just the United Kingdom and the United States, a fact that some say undermined its success.

Saab automotive grew out of the Swedish aircraft industry, and began production in 1949. It was an innovative company, one of the first car makers to introduce the turbocharger and front-wheel design. That and its streamlined, quirky design and reputation for safety won enthusiastic fans and loyal customers.

In 1989, the U.S. firm General Motors (GM) took a 50 percent stake and then bought the company outright in 2000. Under GM's ownership, Saab never turned a profit. Some observers say the company was starved for investment, which greatly restricted its ability to keep up with the market and produce profit-making new models.

In 2010, GM sold Saab to Spyker, a Dutch company, but Saab nevertheless fell into bankruptcy. In 2012, it was sold to a newly-formed company, National Electric Vehicle Sweden (NEVS), a partnership between a Chinese company and a Japanese investment firm, with the purpose of producing Saabs as electric cars. However, in 2014, NEVS also declared bankruptcy.

Is Saab gone for good? Its original parent company, now called the Saab Group, still exists as an aerospace and defense company—building aircraft, air traffic control systems, radar, and other related systems—with headquarters in Stockholm. But the Saab car brand appears to be dead … though, as yet, not quite buried. As long as replacement parts are available, loyal owners will keep their used cars on the road.

Sweden is one of the world's biggest importers of steel. The domestic steel industry specializes in producing high-grade iron and steel for products such as ball bearings, razor blades, and watch and valve springs. About one-third of ordinary steel products are used in construction, shipbuilding, and other industries.

CHEMICALS The chemical industry accounts for about 13 percent of industrial output in Sweden. Growth sectors within that field include organic chemicals, plastics, and pharmaceuticals.

The pharmaceutical industry exports 80 to 90 percent of its output and spends more money than any other industrial sector on research and development. Pharmaceutical research covers genetic engineering, drugs for heart disease, and eye surgery.

Biotechnology expertise includes plant breeding, wastewater treatment, metal extraction, and processes for making plastics and other chemicals. More recently, petrochemicals, a branch of organic chemistry, has been a growing section of the chemical industry.

The forestry industry employs about 4,000 people in Norrbotten, a county in which forest covers about 40 percent of the land.

FORESTRY

More than half of Sweden's land area is forested. The forestry industry is economically important to this country; it employs about 150,000 people and is the principal economic activity in many regions.

The forestry industry produces paper, paperboard, pulp, sawn timber, and other wood products. It is dominated by large companies with their own forests, transportation facilities, and manufacturing plants. The Swedish lumber industry is the largest in Western Europe, producing about 3.5 percent of the world output. Sweden's wood is exported mostly to Great Britain, Germany, Denmark, and the Netherlands.

Blue and yellow, the Swedish national colors, are also the colors of IKEA, a Swedish home furnishings store that seems to have taken over the world. This is not a coincidence. The name IKEA itself is an acronym for the name and hometown of its Swedish founder, Ingvar Kamprad, who started the company as a mail-order business in 1943 when he was only seventeen years old. Today he is one of the wealthiest people on Earth.

An IKEA store in Almhult, Sweden, the hometown of company founder Ingvar Kamprad.

In 2014, IKEA had 349 stores in forty-three countries; with thirty-seven in the United States. The huge warehouse-style stores sell stylish but inexpensive appliances and furniture, much of it to be self-assembled. The IKEA model redefined the home furnishings market and made attractive furniture affordable.

Many of the stores are open long hours and feature a play area for children, a cafeteria serving inexpensive meals of Swedish meatballs, and a Swedish foods section, along with the main showroom for its approximately 12,000 items. The company, which uses some 1 percent of the world's wood in its products, strives to be environmentally conscious in its production and materials.

AGRICULTURE

Only 7 percent of Sweden's land is cultivated for agriculture. Most of the farms and cultivated land are privately owned, and work is carried out mainly by families. Less than 1.1 percent of the labor force is engaged in agriculture. Although resources devoted to agriculture are small, it is nevertheless a vital activity. Swedish farmers use improved irrigation methods, fertilizers, and high-yield seeds to get the best agricultural output. In the warmer south, crops include wheat, sugar beets, potatoes, oil seeds, and peas. In central Sweden, cereals, fodder grain, and plants that yield oil are cultivated. In the colder north, where the growing season is shorter, animal fodder, vegetables, and seed potatoes are grown.

An aerial view shows the farmland around Malmö.

INTERNET LINKS

sweden.se/business
The business section of the Sweden.se site has a wealth of information about its economy, companies, and innovations.

globaledge.msu.edu/countries/sweden/economy
Global Edge offers economic statistics relating to Sweden's economy.

www.washingtonpost.com/business/economy/five-economic-lessons-from-sweden-the-rock-star-of-the-recovery/2011/06/21/AGyuJ3iH_story.html
"Five economic lessons from Sweden, the rock star of the recovery" is an in-depth story from *The Washington Post*.

ENVIRONMENT

A young moose bull is at home in Sarek National Park, in the Laponian Area of Sweden.

5

SWEDEN IS A GLOBAL LEADER WHEN it comes to environmental protection because, in general, they "practice what they preach." Swedes want the world's future generations to enjoy a safe, clean, and beautiful natural environment. They are prepared to lead the way in adopting tough measures to change bad habits and enforcing tough penalties for those who resist. From the Environment Code to the Right of Common Access, Sweden is setting the standard for the rest of world, hoping to spread their love and respect for nature and remind people everywhere of their role as protector of nature.

A 2013 report found Sweden to be the "Most Sustainable Country" in the world. A research firm evaluated and ranked fifty-nine countries on environmental, social, and governing practices relating to environmental policies, emissions, energy use, energy sources, and biodiversity. Sweden came out on top, followed by Australia, Switzerland, Denmark, and Norway. The United States came in ninth.

Small numbers of European lynx live in the Swedish wilderness.

THE FORESTS

Sweden is blessed with extensive forest cover: pine and coniferous forests in the northern region and deciduous forests of oak, elm, ash, hazelnut, and beech in the south. Some of Sweden's many wild plants and flowers, such as poppies, pasque flowers, and orchids, are protected by law.

Many animals make their home in these forests. The king of Swedish wildlife is the moose. This majestic mammal, related to the great North American moose, stands more than 6 feet (2 m) tall. Moose are abundant in most of Sweden except in the far north. The summer population is between 300,000 and 400,000.

Smaller inhabitants of Sweden's forests include roe and fallow deer. Most of the country's predators are not as abundant as its population of deer. Wolves number only between 400 and 500; wolverines total around 650. Their numbers are linked, as wolverines scavenge food killed by wolves. Both animals are protected by law.

Sweden's most common predator is the red fox, and its largest is the brown bear, weighing up to 772 pounds (350 kg). The lynx is Sweden's only wild cat. There are only about 1,250 lynx and 3,500 brown bears living wild in the remote areas of the country, where some counties allow limited hunting of these animals. Southern Sweden is home to more than 300,000 wild boars.

ANIMALS OF THE AIR AND WATER

With the longest coastline in Europe at 4,536 miles (7,300 km) and thousands of inland lakes, Sweden is home to numerous fish and birds. Nevertheless, birds of prey such as eagles and hawks are limited in numbers. Hunting them is prohibited, and efforts are being made to protect the wetlands, which are so critical to the survival of many bird species.

THE ARCTIC FOX

One of the most endangered animals in Sweden is the arctic fox. These white or gray-blue foxes live above the Arctic Circle in a circumpolar territory, meaning around the pole, on the northern edges of Greenland, Russia, Canada, as well as in subarctic alpine regions of Iceland, Norway, Sweden, and Finland.

Although the arctic fox population is not endangered worldwide, it is at critically low levels in Norway, Sweden, and Finland. The total number of adult foxes in those three countries is thought to only be around 120 animals.

Hunting was once the main danger, as the animals were valued for their fur. A century ago, hunting decimated the population in these countries. That threat has diminished somewhat, but indigenous people still hunt the fox as a game species, though governments are taking steps to protect the species.

The growing threat is the incursion of the larger and more aggressive red fox, which is encroaching on the arctic fox's territory as climate change warms the lands where the animals' territories overlap.

The inland lakes support large populations of salmon, capable of growing to more than 38 pounds (17 kg) in weight. Salmon fishing has a long tradition in Sweden, where it is a favorite food which plays an important role in the diet. Anglers need a license to fish for salmon.

About ten thousand gray seals live in Sweden's Baltic waters. Sweden works with its neighbors to protect the Baltic gray seal from poachers who hunt it for its fur. Gray seals give birth in the winter or autumn, and the pups are a target for poachers because of their fluffy white coat. Another water mammal is the otter, with more than two thousand living in the rivers and along the coast in marine environments.

ENVIRONMENTAL CONCERNS

Environmental problems in Sweden come from industrial, agricultural, and consumer waste. From years of fertilizing farmland, Sweden's rivers and lakes contain large quantities of nitrogen and phosphorous washed into the water system by runoff. This abundance of nutrients has resulted in the rapid growth of algae, which depletes the shallow waters of oxygen in the summer. This phenomenon, called eutrophication, also affects the nearby Baltic Sea.

An algal bloom in the water of Långsjön Lake in Holo, Sweden, near Stockholm, is an indicator of pollution.

Heavy industries often release sulfur dioxide into the air; when mixed with rainwater, sulfur dioxide turns into acid rain, which burns plants and makes water systems unfit for fish and animal life. It is difficult to control sulfur dioxide emissions as they do not stay within national boundaries; emissions from northern Europe and southern Sweden combine to damage Sweden's northern lakes and forests.

Another environmental concern in Sweden is global warming from the emission of greenhouse gases produced from burning fossil fuels such as oil and gas. In recent years, this issue has received significant attention by the public and the public officials of Sweden. Sweden ranked as the second best country after Brazil in addressing greenhouse gas emissions and policy formulation.

NATURE LOVERS

Swedish love and respect for nature materialized into serious efforts to protect the environment in the 1970s, when the Swedes realized that the country's beautiful forests and lakes were being destroyed by heavy industry.

Sweden has become a leader in implementing environmental laws and controls. One of the country's main concerns when debating whether to join the European Union (EU) was whether it would be able to continue its environmental reforms. Sweden was concerned that other members of the Union might resist the high standards of environmental protection Sweden wished to maintain.

Today, 48 percent of Sweden's energy use comes from renewable sources, the highest percentage in the EU. The government hopes to hit the 50 percent mark by 2020.

ECONOMIC METHODS

Sweden is a case study in environmental regulation that proves that economic methods can work well. For example, making companies with high sulfur emissions pay a higher tax than companies with reduced emissions brought emissions down by around 80 percent between 1980 and 1996. A tax on nitrogen oxide, a by-product of incineration plants, also reduced emissions by 80 percent from pre-tax levels. A CO_2 tax is having a similar effect on the country's production of this harmful greenhouse gas.

Pollution doesn't just affect urban areas. Farmers try to use the least harmful fertilizers and pesticides.

Farmers are not exempted; they must pay a tax for the use of chemical fertilizers and pesticides. These taxes have funded projects to help clean up farm waste.

Municipalities charge a waste disposal tax to encourage people to reduce the amount of garbage they produce. Manufacturers are legally responsible for collecting and recycling drink bottles, tires, and some forms of packaging. These methods have helped Sweden generate less pollution and keep the use of harmful substances at lower than normal levels for an industrial country.

THE RIGHT OF COMMON ACCESS

The Swedes believe in the right of the individual to enjoy the beauty of nature. They have a common agreement: all open and natural spaces should be accessible to all people at all times. This right dates back centuries and is not legal but moral. Swedes know and

understand this rule and do not need to be told by law or the government how it works. Tour guides are required to explain the right of common access to non-Swedish visitors. This right means that the natural environment is everyone's concern, no matter where they live or what they do.

   ACCESS *The right of common access gives people permission to do certain things on all open, noncultivated land and private roads: walk, cycle, ride a horse, or ski; pick nonprotected wild flowers, berries, mushrooms, fallen pine cones, acorns, and beechnuts; camp or park a trailer for twenty-four hours; let their pets run free; make a campfire; and bathe or boat on open water courses and use the water to drink.*

   RESPONSIBILITY *The right of common access also demands that everyone act responsibly and follow certain guidelines. People are expected not to damage or pollute the land or water; not to enter farms, plantations, or private gardens near people's homes; not to use a motorized vehicle on private lands unless the owner gives permission; not to pick flowers or uproot plants that are protected by law; not to let their pets run free in private hunting lands; and not to make a fire where or when it may cause damage.*

ENVIRONMENTAL GOALS

In 1998 the Environmental Code was enacted by Parliament. This powerful legislation replaced fifteen other environmental laws, which were often confusing and contradictory, with a single national plan and set of regulations.

The goal of the code is to achieve ecological sustainability by 2020 to 2025. Its sixteen environmental quality objectives include reduced climate impact, clean air, a non-toxic environment, sustainable forests, and other goals.

The Swedish Environmental Protection Agency has been charged with coordinating and following up efforts to achieve those objectives. This is an ambitious goal that will require many changes in industry, farming, and everyday living. The hope is that the Environmental Code will create a sustainable economy and lifestyle for the Swedes.

INTERNET LINKS

www.nina.no/portals/0/innholdssider/fjellrev/the%20arctic%20 fox.pdf
"The Arctic Fox" is a colorful, in-depth booklet about the species, its population status, and measures to protect it in Scandinavia.

sweden.se/nature
Sweden.se's "Nature" section offers stories about animals, environmental policy, sustainability, animals, and weather.

www.swedishepa.se
The site of the Swedish Environmental Protection Agency has information about national parks, environmental news, and a video about its environmental policies.

SWEDES

Autumn leaves fall on a young descendant of ancient Germanic tribes.

SWEDES ARE TALL, BLUE-EYED blondes with fair skin—except for the many Swedes who aren't. Most native Swedes are descended from Germanic tribes that came to Scandinavia thousands of years ago. While many Swedes fit the image of the tall fair-skinned blonde, the arrival of immigrants from many parts of the world in the twentieth- and twenty-first centuries has given Sweden a more ethnically diverse population. Today, about 27 percent of Swedes are either immigrants themselves or have an immigrant parent.

DEMOGRAPHICS

The first complete population census, taken in 1749, counted 1.8 million people. The number rose to 3.5 million in 1850 and 7 million in 1950. Today, Sweden's population stands at 9.7 million.

6

In 2013, the number of people from the United States who immigrated to Sweden was 19,010.

Sweden's population is very unevenly distributed. Most Swedes live in the southern part of the country. About 85 percent of the population lives in urban communities, with the cities being the main centers of population—especially Stockholm; Göteborg on the west coast; and Malmö in the south.

PEOPLE ON THE MOVE

In May, people relax in the sun by a pond and blossoming cherry trees in a park in Stockholm.

Between the 1850s and 1930, Sweden experienced a wave of mass emigration. A growing population, the lack of work, and poverty created social problems. Harvest failures and famine between 1853 and 1873 drove out about 103,000 people, or 3 percent of the population. Most went to the United States, settling mainly in Minnesota, Nebraska, and Wisconsin.

Between 1879 and 1893, after a continued economic slump in Sweden and a boom in the United States, about 34,000 Swedes emigrated each year to North America.

By 1900 the Swedish economy had fallen below that of Norway. About 1.5 million people left Sweden between the 1850s and 1930. Some 80 percent of these went to North America, the rest to other Nordic countries. Many stayed for good in their new homeland, while about one-quarter of the emigrants eventually returned.

Post-World War II industrial expansion created a great demand for immigrant labor, and Swedish companies actively recruited from other European countries. In the 1950s, the Nordic countries set up a common labor market, allowing citizens of one Nordic country to work or study in another. In 1967, Sweden introduced immigration controls, leading to a drop in the number of immigrants. Nevertheless, people continue to immigrate to Sweden, attracted by its comfortable lifestyle, freedom, and economic opportunity.

Starting in May 2012, Sweden's population increased by around 0.85 percent. Population growth contributed to this percentage with an increase of 32,676. Immigrants brought another 43,645 people to Sweden, while only 19,592 people emigrated from Sweden.

POPULATION TRENDS

Sweden has an aging population, with an average age of about forty-one years. With quality health care and high living standards, older people are living longer. Sweden now has a life expectancy of 83.6 years for women and 78.8 years for men.

Nevertheless, Sweden also has a good proportion of young people. Children under the age of fourteen account for 17 percent of the population. Sweden has a birth rate of 11.9 babies born per 1000 population, one of the highest in Europe.

An older couple relaxes among the rhododendron in a park in Ronneby

A Sami couple, Britt Marie and Per Nils, wear traditional clothing at home in Soppero.

THE SAMI

The Sami are a minority people who live in the arctic regions of Scandinavia. Historians think the Sami came in nomadic groups from central Russia during pre-Christian times, traveling through southern Finland and settling in northern Scandinavia.

There is no official census, but it's estimated that some 80,000 Sami live in the Finnish-Scandinavian arctic region and along the mountains on both sides of the Swedish-Norwegian border. About 20,000 Sami live in Sweden and vary in their commitment to their culture. Some Sami identify themselves strongly as a separate ethnic group, while others have been assimilated into Swedish culture.

The Samis' traditional occupation was breeding reindeer. However, today, only 10 percent of Swedish Sami earn a living from the reindeer industry. The importance of reindeer breeding can be seen in the way breeders belong to a village, which serves not just as a grazing area but also an administrative unit. Common facilities are built and maintained by the village, and the cost is shared among the residents.

Over the years, the Sami have given up their nomadic lifestyle for permanent settlements in the low fell region, where mountain reindeer mate and reproduce. However, reindeer breeding is not very profitable, as a herd of at least 500 is needed to earn enough money for the family.

In Jokkmokk, in Swedish Lappland, high school students work on handicrafts in a class that focuses on Sami culture.

Many Sami families supplement their income by hunting, fishing, selling handicrafts, and hosting tourists. Sami handicrafts made from traditional materials can be found at the winter market fair in Jokkmokk. The Samis' traditional food is reindeer meat and milk and cheese made from reindeer milk. One delicacy is *lappkok* (LAHP-shehk), a broth of reindeer marrow bones and shredded liver.

The Sami language belongs to the Finno-Ugric group and has three dialects. The most widely used is North Sami, spoken in northern Sweden, Norway, and the far north of Finland. South Sami is spoken in north-central Sweden and central Norway. East Sami is spoken in eastern Finland and the Kola Peninsula in Russia.

Sami children go to a regular state-supported school or a state-run nomad school. Both have the same aims, except that the nomad school includes the teaching of Sami language and culture. Children in regular schools learn their language and culture at home through a special home language project.

Without a strong written tradition, Sami culture has been passed down orally in a form of singing called *jojking* (YOI-king).

More than four hundred types of folk clothing are worn in Sweden. Originally peasant attire, these are now worn on festive occasions or as formal wear, no longer for the same functions or with the same significance as before.

Each traditional outfit is recognizable through the type of fabric used, the embroidery, and the accessories, among other things. Not all folk outfits today are exact replicas of those worn in past centuries; many have been redesigned with a modern twist.

There are many elements to the complete folk outfit, and there are strict rules for wearing it correctly. A woman's traditional outfit usually consists of a white cotton or linen blouse with long, sometimes puffy, sleeves; a skirt, embroidered at the hem and gathered at the waist; a vest, apron, shawl, and bonnet or hat; a purse; silver jewelry; and stockings and shoes.

In the nineteenth century, Karin Larsson, wife of Swedish painter Carl Larsson, designed a national folk dress for women that included a blue skirt with a yellow apron, and a red bodice embroidered with white daisies.

A man's traditional outfit consists of a long-sleeved white cotton shirt, a vest, knee-length trousers, and knee-high stockings. A rimmed hat and a knee-length embroidered coat may top off the outfit. A hat band or braid indicates whether the man is married or single.

Unmarried girls in some regions braid their hair and bind it with a red band or wear an open-ended bonnet, while in other regions, they do not cover their hair. Married women traditionally keep their heads covered all the time, with a white linen bonnet or a stiff frame cap. The headgear indicates whether the woman is going to a festive occasion or a sad one.

SWEDEN'S CHANGING FACE

Since World War II, immigrants have played an increasingly important role in Sweden. Being a neutral country during the war, Sweden welcomed refugees from other Nordic and Baltic states. Many returned home after the war, but some remained as there was a demand for labor. Many immigrants also came from Finland, Norway, and Denmark when an agreement was signed in 1954 creating a common labor market among these countries.

Makeshift shelters of migrants and asylum seekers from Europe and the Middle East form a temporary encampment on a forested hillside in Stockholm in February 2014.

In the 1960s, Sweden experienced two big waves of immigration due to growing industrialization. The first wave, in the mid-1960s, saw the arrival of workers from former Yugoslavia, Greece, Italy, Germany, Turkey, and Poland. The second wave took place between 1968 and 1970, with most immigrants coming from Finland.

As the economy slowed down in the 1970s, so did the inflow of foreign workers. The government also took steps to restrict immigration.

A decade ago, most immigrants were political refugees from Slovenia, Romania, Chile, Iran, Iraq, Somalia, and Ethiopia. More recently, in the twenty-first century, most immigrants have come from war-torn Muslim countries, such as Iraq, Afghanistan, and Somalia. The government has introduced measures to help integrate newcomers into Swedish society. These aim to establish equality between immigrants and Swedes, freedom of cultural choice and cooperation, and solidarity between the Swedish majority and the various ethnic minorities.

INTEGRATING IMMIGRANTS

Burned out cars in a suburb of Stockholm remain after youths rioted in response to a police action in an immigrant neighborhood in May 2013.

Some thirty national immigration organizations have been set up through government grants to give minority groups a collective voice. There are foreign language newspapers to keep the immigrant population informed of events in Sweden.

Language programs for newly arrived adults include courses in Swedish and are paid for by the government. There are also home language programs for immigrant children to learn their native language to help preserve Sweden's ethnic cultures.

Also significant is the right of foreigners who have lived in Sweden for at least three years to vote and run for office in local and regional elections. Non-citizens have the same rights as Swedes with regard to social benefits and education.

Nevertheless, the integration of people from different cultures has brought some tension in some Swedish communities. Immigrants bring with them their own particular ways of life, including their opinions and prejudices.

For example, the recent influx of Muslim people escaping violence in their own lands has also brought an increase in violence against Jews living in Sweden, especially around Malmö in the south. A Swedish government study in 2006 estimated that 5 percent of the total adult population and 39 percent of adult Muslims hold "systematic antisemitic views." The situation became so grave that in 2010, the Simon Wiesenthal Center, a Jewish human rights organization, issued a travel advisory alerting Jews to an increase in verbal and physical harassment of Jewish citizens in the Swedish city of Malmö.

INTERNET LINKS

worldpopulationreview.com/countries/sweden-population
This page gives a clear overview of the Swedish population statistics.

www.samer.se/2137
"The Sami—An Indigenous People in Sweden" is a 65-page PDF booklet with a wealth of information and photographs produced by the Swedish government and the National Sami Information Centre.

www.goteborgdaily.se/news/swedes-concerned-about-growing-racism
This article from *Goteborg Daily* includes links to related articles about immigrants and attitudes in Sweden.

www.businessinsider.com/sweden-politics-immigration-and-population-ageing-present-policy-challeng-2012-8
"Sweden Will Have To Become A Lot Less Blond" looks at the impact of immigration in Sweden.

www.foreverswedish.net/folk-draumlkt.html
Forever Swedish has a nice section on folk dress.

LIFESTYLE

Commuters make their way home at the end of the work day in Gamla Stan, the old city in Stockholm.

SWEDES ARE HARDWORKING people. Many believe that hard work is essential to support a welfare state, and they are right. They are punctual and efficient; and work, on average, about 1,644 hours per year. Swedes tend not to overwork themselves or feel they must work long hours into the night to prove their worth to their boss. Swedes tend to value teamwork and it wouldn't be appropriate for one person to be so ambitious for his or her own sake.

What do Swedes aspire to? What's the "Swedish Dream"? The answer is summed up in three V's: *villa, Volvo, vovve* ("a house, a Volvo and a dog").

Swedes live according to a concept called *lagom*. There is no English word for it, but it means something like "just right," "adequate," or "as needed." It can also mean "in balance," or "perfect simple." Lagom means doing, having, or being the best amount of whatever it is, but no more. The concept frowns on wasteful excess or any kind of "too much": overeating, drinking, or working; excessive consumerism—having too much stuff—or even extreme emotionalism.

THE STATE PROVIDES

The way of life for the average Swede is to a large extent defined by the welfare state, which provides basic social, educational, and medical

Nursery school children work with iPads.

services ranging from the district doctor to daily child-care. Users of these services pay a small fee according to how much they earn.

To finance the welfare state, Swedes pay some of the highest income taxes in the world. These high taxes have been a heavy burden, and politically there is occasional backlash. Nevertheless, most Swedish people support the system and feel they are getting their money's worth.

EDUCATION

Every Swedish child has access to formal education, regardless of his or her parents' income. There are a few private schools, but the majority of children attend state-run schools. All Swedish children are required to complete twelve years of compulsory education.

Most children start school at age seven, but they can start at age six if their parents prefer. Children spend nine years in *grundskola* (GROOND-skol-lah), a comprehensive school program divided into three stages: lower school (grades one to three), middle school (grades four to six), and upper school (grades seven to nine). Grades one to six are the equivalent of elementary and middle school in the United States. All children learn the same subjects in grades one to six, with English introduced in grade three. When they reach grade seven, they can choose the courses they want to study.

After grade nine, children must attend three years at *gymnasium* (gim-NAH-sium), or senior high school. At the end of gymnasium, students celebrate with a big graduation party. About one-third of young Swedes go on to study at one of Sweden's more than forty colleges and universities. Students are entitled to apply for a state loan to pay college fees, and this is repaid after graduation, upon getting a job.

CARING FOR CHILDREN

For most Swedes with children, the day begins with dropping the children off at a child-care center or at school before going to work. About 60 percent of preschool children attend a *daghem* (DAHG-hem), or day-care center. When they start school, they still go to the day-care center after school is over and wait for their parents to pick them up after work.

Children in daycare take a walk with their caretakers in the upscale Ostermalm neighborhood of Stockholm.

Sweden's well-developed system of child-care centers has allowed Swedish women to work outside the home. At the same time, the high cost of living and high taxes mean that both partners must work so that the family can live comfortably.

The welfare state offers several benefits to the people so that they can combine work with having a family. When a young couple has a child, they make use of generous paid leave offered in no other country. Under Swedish law, parents are entitled to a total of 480 days per child, which they can take any time until the child is eight years old. The parents can share these days, although sixty are given specifically to the father. During that time, they are entitled to 80 percent of their wages, up to a certain amount.

In addition, the government provides an additional monthly child allowance until a child is 16. In 2013, the allowance was 1,050 kroner (about $152) per month per child.

Swedes love children, and they have taken great pains to ensure that children's rights are protected. Swedish children have their own government ombudsman to look after their interests. The child ombudsman reports cases of abuse of minors to the social welfare committee, which investigates and intervenes where necessary. In 1979, Sweden was the first country in the world to outlaw the corporal punishment of children—that is, the spanking, hitting, paddling, or beating of children—at home, at school, or anywhere. Eventually, thirty other countries followed Sweden's example.

GENDER EQUALITY

Sweden is a society with few class differences. It is difficult to notice any distinction between the working class and the middle class. In the 1960s, fast economic growth brought about a uniformly high standard of living, distributing income around the country. Today, the income gap between skilled and unskilled workers is relatively narrow, and the tax system further closes this gap.

Attention is now focused on establishing equality between men and women. The government has tried to help both men and women to attain economic independence. Steps have been taken to make it easier for women to hold a job as well as have a family. Women make up half the Swedish labor force, and it is rare for someone to be without a job, whether part-time or full-time, even if they have children.

It is not surprising that Sweden has the highest rate of working women in Europe. The state encourages young mothers to continue working by granting long periods of paid leave to both parents when a child is born and by funding quality care facilities for children once they reach their first birthday. Most women go back to work after their maternity leave.

However, many occupations pay women less than they pay men, although the wage differential is small compared with other countries. Steps have been taken to give women more choices, but they continue to bear more responsibility than do men in taking care of the children and the domestic chores.

HELPING THE ELDERLY

Sweden is an aging country. Eighteen percent of Swedes are age 65 or older, and that figure is expected to rise to 30 percent by 2030. Services for elderly are available from both public and private sources, funded by municipal taxes and government grants. Sweden spends more of its money (as measured by gross domestic product) on its elderly than any other country in the world.

More than 90 percent of elderly Swedes live in ordinary homes, some modified to meet their needs. Without a younger relative living with them, many elderly use home-help services for their daily chores, such as shopping, cleaning, and cooking. District doctors and nurses make home calls to treat ill or housebound elderly. At the same time, municipalities run centers where the elderly get the opportunity to meet others and socialize.

Old people who are fairly fit can choose to live in service houses, apartment buildings that are owned and managed by the municipality. Residents at service houses enjoy subsidized home help and facilities such as a restaurant and activity rooms. Those who are less able to care for themselves live in old-age homes where 24-hour care is provided. Such homes, however, are being phased out as more state support is given for the elderly in their own residences.

Karl Erik Wettergren, 93, and Margareta Nordin, 92, work out during their weekly fitness class at a health club outside Stockholm.

MARRIAGE AND COHABITATION

Cohabitation, or living together without being married, is a common living arrangement in Sweden. The Swedish word for living together is *samboende* (SAHM-boh-ehn-deh) or *sambo*, which also refers to the person one is living with. Many unmarried couples who live together have children; there are also single-parent families. In 2012, 54.5 percent of Swedish children were born to unmarried parents. This trend is not unique to Sweden; similar statistics are found in other Scandinavian and European countries.

Nevertheless, Sweden has one of the lowest marriage rates in the industrialized world. One couple in five lives together—five times the number in the United States. At the same time, many married couples in Sweden eventually separate. The country has one of the highest divorce rates in

Europe; about 50 percent of Swedish marriages end in divorce. Many couples in Sweden choose to live together as a temporary measure, postponing marriage until both partners are more settled in their jobs. Often, children attend their parents' wedding.

Same-sex marriage has been legal since 2009, when the Swedish parliament passed it by an overwhelming majority. Previously, gay couples in Sweden had been able to register for civil unions since 1995. The 2009 law allows gays and lesbians to marry in both religious and civil ceremonies. However, it does not require clergy to officiate at such ceremonies. The Church of Sweden, a Lutheran denomination, has offered blessings for same-sex partnerships since 2007. In 2009, the year the law was changed, the church's governing board voted to allow its clergy to officiate at same-sex marriage ceremonies. About 75 percent of Swedes belong to the Church of Sweden.

CITY LIFE, COUNTRY LIFE

A few generations ago, most of Sweden's population was rural. Industrialization in the twentieth century pulled many Swedes away from their farms and villages and to the cities. Today, about 85 percent of Sweden's population lives in urban areas, although Swedes still like the country life. Many city people own vacation homes in the country where they can take a break from the rush of the city to enjoy the country life.

NAMES

Swedish names can sound so similar that sometimes it is difficult to distinguish them. Until a century ago, many Swedish families did not have surnames. A person had a given name and a father's first name. Peter, whose father's name was John, was "Peter John's son," or Peter Johnson. His sister Greta was Greta Johndotter. Their father might have been "John Carl's son," or John Carlson.

Today, everyone has a first and a family name. But since many surnames end in *-son*, the phone book might list hundreds of John Carlsons. So phone books specify the person's occupation to distinguish John Carlson the teacher from John Carlson the engineer.

INTERNET LINKS

www.endcorporalpunishment.org/pages/pdfs/ending.pdf
"Ending Corporal Punishment" is a PDF of a booklet published by the Swedish Ministry of Health and Social Affairs reviewing Sweden's no-spanking policy.

www.nytimes.com/2010/06/10/world/europe/10iht-sweden.html?pagewanted=all&_r=0
The New York Times article "In Sweden, Men Can Have It All" examines parental leave for men.

sciencenordic.com/increased-divorce-rates-are-linked-welfare-state
ScienceNordic's article "Increased divorce rates are linked to the welfare state" examines the reasons for Sweden's high divorce rate.

RELIGION

A rose window of stained glass lights the interior of a cathedral in Uppsala.

8

SWEDEN IS A MOSTLY CHRISTIAN country in which people have freedom of religion, which also means freedom from religion. By tradition, most Swedes belong to the Lutheran Church of Sweden, but in practice, many are not particularly religious. Compared with the United States, and in fact with most of the world, the Scandinavian countries are quite secular. Most people take a very relaxed attitude toward their religion, or simply don't practice it at all.

Early Christianity in Sweden was of the Roman Catholic faith. After splitting away from Norway and Denmark, Gustav Vasa reduced the economic power of the Roman Catholic Church in Sweden. In 1527 he started the Protestant Reformation at Västerås. Olaus Petri, an Örebro native who had been inspired by Martin Luther and other European reformers, and his brother, Laurentius Andreae, the king's chancellor, were the driving force behind the Reformation in Sweden.

Citing the increasing ethnic diversity and secularization of Sweden, on January 1, 2000, the Swedish government ended the designation of Lutheranism as the official state religion after nearly five hundred years.

THE REFORMATION

Olaus Petri contributed to Swedish Protestantism in many ways. He prepared a hymnbook, a church manual, and liturgy for the people and helped translate the Bible into Swedish.

In 1544, Sweden became a Protestant country when it was officially proclaimed a Lutheran kingdom. The king became head of the Church of Sweden. Some Roman Catholic priests left Sweden rather than accept Protestantism; others stayed and, together with the people, gradually accepted Protestantism. Roman Catholics later attempted to regain power but failed.

Lutheranism became more firmly established in Sweden during the reign of Gustavus II Adolphus (1611—32). In the eighteenth and nineteenth centuries, however, the Pietism revival movement swept the Lutheran Church, as people turned to home Bible sharing and prayer and fellowship in small groups for a deeper, more personal religious experience.

A statue of Olaus Petri stands in front of Storkyrkan (the Church of St. Nicholas). Dating from the thirteenth century, it is the oldest church in Gamla Stan, the old town in central Stockholm.

LUTHERANISM

The origins of the Lutheran Church go back to Martin Luther, the sixteenth-century German monk and Roman Catholic priest. He objected to some Catholic practices and started a movement known as the Protestant Reformation. Through his actions and writings, he ushered in not only Protestantism, but also a seedbed for new economic, political, and social thought.

Like all Christians, Lutherans believe in the divinity and humanity of Jesus Christ and in the Trinity of God. They have two sacraments: Baptism and the Lord's Supper (Communion). Lutherans believe in salvation through

faith alone, rather than through good works. The basic unit of government in the Lutheran Church is the congregation. It is led by either a pastor or a lay person elected from the membership of a council, which is made up of a congregation's clergy and elected lay persons.

Until 1991, the Church of Sweden was responsible for maintaining population records, which it had done since the seventeenth century. Until the latter half of the eighteenth century, all Swedes were expected to be a part of the Church of Sweden. In 1781, the Edict of Toleration was issued, allowing other religious groups to practice their faith in the country. Full religious freedom was guaranteed by law only in 1952.

Unlike in some other Christian churches, the Church of Sweden has been ordaining women ministers since 1958.

THE CHURCH OF SWEDEN TODAY

The Lutheran Church of Sweden is still the dominant faith in the country and, as of 2013, was professed by about 66 percent of the population. Despite its large church membership, Sweden is basically a secular state, and religion

A statue of Bridget of Sweden in Vadstenas Abbey on Lake Vättern dates to 1425.

plays a minor role in the lives of most Swedes. According to one poll in 2010, just 18 percent of Swedish respondents said that "they believe there is a god," though 45 percent said "they believe there is some sort of spirit or life force." In another poll, 17 percent answered yes to the question "Is religion an important part of your daily life?" Only about 4 percent of the population attends church regularly.

Swedes generally keep Christian customs by marrying in church, getting their children baptized and confirmed, and holding church funeral services. More than 70 percent of babies are baptized and 90 percent of funerals are performed by the Church of Sweden.

OTHER CHURCHES

The Roman Catholic Church has the second largest congregation in Sweden, with about 2 percent of the population. Recent immigrants from Slavic and Latin American countries have boosted its membership.

There are a few Protestant denominations in Sweden besides the Lutheran Church. Known as the "free churches," these include other Protestant denominations as well as the Pentecostal movement, which gained prominence in the early twentieth century in the United States and has since spread rapidly to other parts of the world. Free Church members number about 250,000.

Pentecostal services are enthusiastic and rousing, with an emphasis on music and lively congregational participation. Pentecostal churches are attractive to people who are interested in social reforms and an alternative to the orthodoxy of the Church of Sweden.

The second largest Protestant denomination in Sweden, Pentecostal churches are still growing in membership, the fastest growing religious movement in the country.

Another growing Protestant denomination is the Mission Covenant Church of Sweden, with approximately 65,000 members. Some of Sweden's

Protestant churches were founded as a reaction to the perceived rigidity of the Church of Sweden, while others were imported from other countries.

OTHER RELIGIONS

Close to half a million Muslims form the largest group of non-Christians in Sweden, making up about 5 percent of the population. Swedish Muslims are mainly immigrants from Turkey, the Middle East, and North Africa.

Sweden's third largest religious group is the Jews, who have had congregations in Sweden for more than two centuries. There are also small numbers of Buddhists, Hindus, and Jehovah's Witnesses.

A mosque in the southern Swedish city of Malmö serves a mostly immigrant population.

INTERNET LINKS

www.nytimes.com/2009/02/28/us/28beliefs.html?pagewanted=all
"Scandinavian Nonbelievers, Which Is Not to Say Atheists" is a *New York Times* article explaining the secularism of Sweden.

www.state.gov/j/drl/rls/irf/2009/127339.htm
The U.S. State Department "International Religious Freedom Report 2009: Sweden" gives an in-depth overview of religious freedom in Sweden.

LANGUAGE

Ancient runestones like this one harken back to the Viking Age. Many of the stones are decorated with serpentine patterns and runic inscriptions.

9

SVENSKA, THE MODERN SWEDISH language, comes from the North Germanic family of languages and is closely related to the Danish, Norwegian, Icelandic, and Faeroese languages. It developed from primitive Norse, the language of the Vikings.

The earliest language source in Sweden can be traced to runic inscriptions. The most common material for runes was wood, none of

A detail of a stone relief shows the divine triad of Norse gods: Odin, the chief god, Thor, the god of thunder, and Freya, the god of fertility.

One study concluded that the Sami languages have around 180 words for snow, describing distinctions in condition. And there are as many as one thousand words for reindeer! But despite the abundance of descriptive words, the languages are genderless: for example, the personal pronoun son can mean *him*, *her*, or *it*.

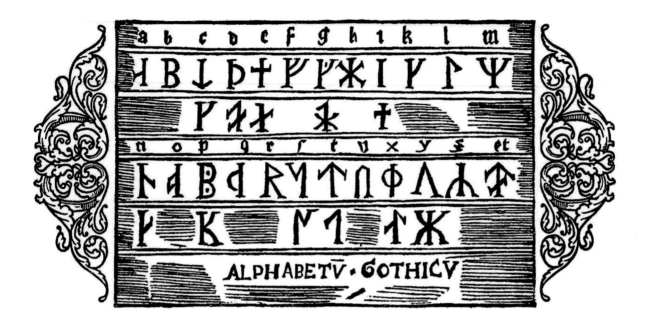

which have been preserved. Runes have also been found on stone, weapons such as spears and blades, and ornaments such as brooches.

RUNESTONES

The earliest runestones are from the eighth century. Little is known about their origin, but they were thought to be linked to magic and sorcery. From these stones, scholars have learned about the political, economic, and cultural aspects of those times.

The symbols on the runestones were usually set within a decorated image of a snake or dragon coil and sometimes included other designs. Stone cutters occasionally added more detail to the commissioned text. Runestones also tell of Viking voyages to faraway Byzantium and Baghdad. Many runestones were erected in memory of famous men who died on such journeys. From these stones we have learned about Viking myths, such as the creation of humans and the exploits of Viking gods such as Sigurd the dragon-slayer. The most famous runestone from the ninth century is the *Rökstone* in Östergötland. It has no ornamental design and contains the longest runic text in the world.

The Runic alphabet is of German origin. It has two systems of alphabet: an older system with twenty-four letters, used from the third to ninth centuries, and a later, simpler alphabet with sixteen letters. The golden age of runic writing was in the eleventh and twelfth centuries, when trade was at its peak.

SVENSKA

The origin of modern Svenska is usually dated from the year 1526, when a Swedish translation of the Bible's New Testament was first printed. Standard Swedish, which emerged in the seventeenth century, is derived mainly from the Svea dialects spoken around Stockholm and Lake Mälaren.

The modern alphabet, the Latin alphabet, was introduced in the thirteenth century through the spread of Christianity. However, the Svenska alphabet does not have the letters *W* or *Z*. Instead it has three other letters, with pronunciation marks: *å*, pronounced like the *o* in the English word *for*; *ä*, which sounds like the *ai* in the English word *fair*; and *ö*, pronounced somewhat like the *u* in the English word *turn*. These three unique Swedish letters come at the very end of the Svenska alphabet.

The Swedish language became more regulated with the arrival of printing and the production of books in the sixteenth century. In 1786 King Gustav III founded the Swedish Academy, whose main goal was to improve the "purity, vigor, and majesty" of the language. In 1836, the Academy published a Swedish grammar book. It now publishes two dictionaries. The eighteen-member Academy, with the motto "Talent and Taste," also awards the Nobel Prize for Literature every year.

SPELLING AND PRONUNCIATION

Swedish spelling and pronunciation differ from English convention. For example, the letter *g* can be pronounced with a hard *g* sound as in *gamla* (GAHM-lah), meaning "ancient," or with a *y* sound as in *Göteborg* (YUE-teh-

A Swedish sign warns drivers to watch for school children.

bory). The letter *j* is pronounced with a *y* sound as in *ja* (yah), meaning "yes," and *mjölk* (myolk), meaning "milk." The letter *k* sounds like *ch*, especially when used with the letters *j* or *y*, as in *kyckling* (CHICK-ling), or "chicken," and the *Kölen* (CHO-len) mountains.

Pronunciation marks also change the sound of letters. Accent marks indicate which syllable is emphasized as well as the pitch, or tone. There are two tones: high, or acute, and low, or grave.

When learning to write Swedish, it is safer to memorize the correct spelling of a word than try to guess by its pronunciation. For example, there is no simple rule for spelling the *sh* sound in Swedish; the *sh* may be left as is or replaced with a *sj* or *sch*.

SIMILARITY TO ENGLISH

To the ear of an English speaker, Swedish sounds vaguely familiar. This is because Swedish and English belong to branches of the same linguistic tree—Germanic. Svenska rose out of the North Germanic branch, while English, German, and Dutch developed from the West Germanic branch.

Some Swedish words sound a lot like English: *moder* (MOH-der), *fader* (FAH-der), *syster* (SIS-ter), *broder* (BROH-der), *student* (stu-DENT), *dörr* (door), and *bok* (book). Translated into English, these words are, of course, "mother, father, sister, brother, student, door, and book." Other Swedish words include *tack* (tahk), meaning "thanks," *tomat* (toh-MAH), or "tomato," and *frukt* (froot), or "fruit."

Modern-day Swedish has adopted many foreign words, mainly from Americanized English. Words like "jeans" and "ketchup" are commonly used by Swedes today. Most Swedes also understand Danish and Norwegian to some degree, since these Scandinavian languages are similar to Swedish.

REGIONAL DIALECTS

There are several regional dialects in Sweden, but these are no longer widely spoken.

Older Swedes, especially those living in more geographically isolated areas in the North, continue to use the dialect of their area. Most young people speak standard Swedish, although with a noticeable regional accent. These accents are so marked that Swedes are able to identify the regional origin of the speaker.

As in many countries, the standard language of Sweden originates from one dialect. Standard Swedish has its roots in a dialect spoken around Lake Mälaren, where Stockholm is. Historically, this province was the center of power and economic activity.

Wooden signs point directions for hikers in Nikkaluokta, Lappland.

INTERNET LINKS

sweden.se/tag/swedish-language
Official site of Sweden: How to learn Swedish.

www.omniglot.com/writing/swedish.htm
Omniglot has a good overview of the Swedish alphabet and pronunciations.

www.svenskaakademien.se/en
The site of the Swedish Academy explains its various functions.

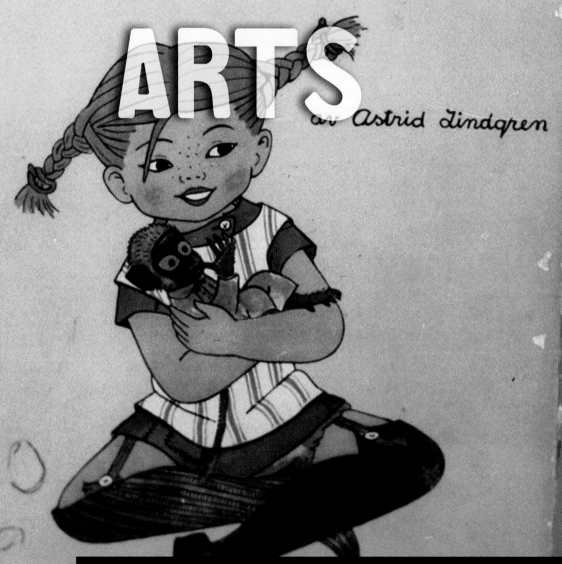

BOKEN OM
PiPPi LÅNGSTRUMP

ARTS

av Astrid Lindgren

The 1946 cover of *Pippi Longstocking* shows one of Sweden's most enduring literary characters.

10

FROM ABBA TO ZORN, SWEDISH ART is an expression of traditional folk heritage and modern, international sophistication. The country boasts some three hundred cultural institutions, including national museums of art, archaeology, natural history, and cultural history; county and municipal museums conserving regional heritage; and folk and other specialized museums.

Sweden is renowned for its blown glasswork. The Kingdom of Crystal (Glasriket), in the province of Småland, is a geographical region containing fifteen glassworks, including the world famous Orrefors and Kosta Boda.

Glassblowing is an important artisan industry in the Kingdom of Crystal region of Småland.

SCANDINAVIAN DESIGN

In Stockholm, a shopper walks past an H&M store, a Swedish shop that sells trendy clothing at low prices.

Swedish aesthetics and democratic ideals play an important role in the Scandinavian design movement that became popular in the 1950s and continues today. Scandinavian design is expressed in home furnishings and everyday objects that are characterized by simplicity, minimalism, modernism, and functionality. The idea is that useful objects can be beautiful, stylish, and—because they are mass produced using low-cost materials—affordable to all.

Sweden's IKEA home furnishings company is a prime example of the Scandinavian design concept, but designers and retailers from Denmark, Finland, and Norway are working in the same vein. Even fashion designers and retailers such as Sweden's H&M reflect the Scandinavian design approach.

ABBA

The greatest music sensation to come out of Sweden—or out of anywhere, really—was the pop group ABBA. It was just about the most successful music group ever, second only to The Beatles. Made up of Agnetha Fältskog, Björn Ulvaeus, Benny Andersson, and Anni-Frid Lyngstad—ABBA is an acronym of the first letters of their first names—the quartet ruled the airwaves from 1972 to 1982 with their catchy dance tunes.

The band sold more than one billion albums and singles, with numerous No. 1 hits overseas. "Dancing Queen," released in 1976, made it to the top of the Billboard Hot 100 in the United States. It is generally considered ABBA's signature song and Rolling Stone magazine rated it number 174 of "The 500 Greatest Songs of All Time." ABBA's other big hits include "Waterloo," "Mamma Mia," and "SOS."

In 1999, ABBA's music was adapted into the hugely successful musical theater production Mamma Mia! To this day, it plays on Broadway and in London and tours worldwide. A movie of the show, released in 2008, became the highest-grossing film in the United Kingdom that year. In 2010, ABBA was inducted into the Rock and Roll Hall of Fame.

SWEDEN ROCKS

Sweden may be cold, but people in the music industry know it's one of the hottest places on Earth. Behind only the United States and the United Kingdom, Sweden is the world's third largest music exporter. Swedish artists make all types of music: rock, heavy metal, indie, pop, electronica, hip-hop, folk, and more. Well-known acts include Ace of Base, Roxette, The Cardigans, Peter Bjorn and John, Avicii, and Robyn, as well as the mega-producer Max Martin, numerous songwriters, and many others in the music business. In May 2012, half of the top ten songs on the Billboard Hot 100 list in the United States were written or produced by Swedes. And then, of course, there's always ABBA.

But there's more to Swedish music than new genres. Old-time music is still alive as well.

FOLK MUSIC Originating in eighteenth- and nineteenth-century peasant society, folk music is still sung and enjoyed by Swedes today. Singing games, in which the singers act out the lyrics, are especially popular with children, who learn the songs from an early age.

Originally, Swedish folk songs were sung without musical accompaniment. Peasants sang as they spun wool, did repairs, and made tools on long, cold winter nights. Some of these songs were long ballads that told a story, others were humorous, and still others were religious in nature. The peasants first learned the songs from books and then sang them to their children.

Fiddlers occupied a special place in folk music. They played at weddings and other festivities where there was dancing. Local melodies were handed down from one fiddler to another. Fiddlers were also looked upon as magical figures. There were stories about magic fiddles and fiddlers taught by *Näcken* ("NECK-kehn"), a wicked water spirit. Fiddlers were even thought to be associated with the devil.

Today, the traditions and enthusiasm for folk music are kept alive through clubs, guilds, and competitions. Annual festivals, such as the Music on Lake Siljan Festival for fiddlers, attract many participants and large audiences.

Musicians play at a traditional folk music festival in Bingsjo.

MUSICAL INSTRUMENTS A revival in folk music has renewed interest in folk instruments, especially those with drones that make low-pitched sounds. These include the bowed harp, bagpipe, hurdy-gurdy, Swedish zither, mouth harp, and older keyed fiddles. The keyed fiddle's drone strings give a characteristic tonal sound. The player uses a bow and stops the strings using keys rather than fingers.

Swedish musicians still use old wind instruments such as the clarinet and wooden flute. The cow horn and a wooden trumpet called the *lur* ("LOOR") are used for herding cattle. Herding music, which consists of calls and signals used for communicating with the animals, is thought to be Sweden's oldest surviving domestic musical tradition.

SAMI MUSIC The music of the Sami, believed to be the oldest form of music in Europe, reflects their nomadic history and way of life. It is very different from Swedish and other European music. The *jojk* ("yoik") is a spontaneous, improvised song that recalls people or places and evokes related emotions. It is a personal song sung without accompaniment. Musical instruments are rarely used in Sami music.

MOVIES

Swedish films have the reputation of being dark and gloomy. Certainly many of Ingmar Bergman's movies fall into that category. Bergman was one of the most famous, and most influential, movie directors in the history of film. He first achieved international fame with *The Seventh Seal* (1956). This was followed by his Oscar-winning *Wild Strawberries* (1957), *Through a Glass Darkly* (1961), *Cries and Whispers* (1972), and *Fanny and Alexander* (1982). Many of his films are bleak meditations on Swedish life and explore the themes of faith and doubt, illness and death, loneliness, betrayal, sex, and insanity. Today, universities worldwide regularly offer film courses on Bergman's art.

However, not all Swedish movies follow the Bergman model. Director Lasse Hallström made his film debut with a comedy and went on to world fame with *My Life as a Dog* and other big name movies. More recently, the films based on *The Girl With the Dragon Tattoo* series have been international hits, as are the novels they are based on.

Sweden has also given the world a number of movie stars and famous actors. In the twentieth century, Greta Garbo, Ingrid Bergman, Max von Sydow, and Ann-Margret were household names. Today, actor Stellan Skarsgård—*The Avengers* (2012), *Good Will Hunting* (1997)—is familiar to U.S. audiences, as is his son Alexander Skarsgård—*Tarzan* (2016), *The Giver* (2014), the HBO series *True Blood* (2008–2014).

Actors Alexander and Stellan Skarsgård arrive for the premiere of *The Avengers* in Los Angeles.

UNDERGROUND ART

Perhaps the best example of art in daily life is found in Stockholm's subway network. More than ninety of the one hundred subway stations in Stockholm have been decorated with sculptures, mosaics, paintings, installations, engravings and reliefs by more than 150 artists. Fantastical works decorate the ticket booths, track walls, platforms, and ceilings, making the capital's subway network "the world's longest art gallery."

The gallery was started in the late 1940s when the subway system was first built. Since then, the colorful "canvas" that makes catching the train every day such a pleasure has been expanded. The different works reflect the spirit of each decade. There is a 60-foot

(18.3-m) human profile in terrazzo, tiles, and cobblestones; platform pillars that have been turned into giant trees; fantasy beetles in glass cases, and even a 315-foot- (96-m-) long photo montage of present-day Sweden. At several of the stations, the bedrock has been left exposed, crude, and unfinished, as part of the art.

"Braskkulla, a Peasant Girl from Moro," is a painting by Anders Zorn.

FINE ARTS

Swedish artists have contributed to the major movements of the Western art world. But art in Sweden is part of everyday life, not just a collection of important paintings housed in a museum. Modern Swedish artists enjoy a strong following, and aspiring painters and sculptors receive training at all levels, from study circles to colleges.

Sweden has its share of internationally well-known painters, such as turn-of-the-century impressionist painter Anders Zorn (1860—1920). Though he painted many subjects, Zorn achieved fame as a portrait painter; he painted three U.S. presidents among other important leaders and high-society figures of the time.

Sweden's most beloved artist is Carl Larrson (1853—1919). His illustrative style captures cozy domestic scenes of ordinary Swedish life, idealized but not glamorized. His paintings often depict his wife Karin and their eight children and the rural community in which they lived. His art is a rich and lovely record of life in rural Sweden more than a century ago.

THEATER

The roots of modern Swedish theater can be traced to the eighteenth century when King Gustavus III opened the doors of his theater to the commoners. Before then, court theaters were available only to the aristocracy. In those days, the actors spoke French instead of Swedish. This was because French was the language of culture in Europe.

Today, Swedes can enjoy a wide range of plays, including classical, modern, children's, and experimental, in the two national theaters—the Opera and the Royal Dramatic Theater in Stockholm.

There are also some municipal theaters in other parts of the country that cater to Swedes living outside the capital. The idea of folk theater, or theater for everyone, gave rise to the touring drama company that helped to popularize this art form in Sweden.

The Palace Theater in Drottningholm

The Drottningholm Court Theater, situated in the premises of the residence of the royal family on the outskirts of Stockholm, was built in the eighteenth century and is believed to be one of the oldest theaters in use today. It stages thirty plays every year and seats only 450 spectators each time. UNESCO declared Drottningholm a World Heritage site in 1992.

FROM AUGUST TO ASTRID

Many Swedish writers have achieved international fame and had their works translated into other languages.

Among the best-known of Sweden's literary figures was August Strindberg (1849–1912), who wrote novels, short stories, poetry, and plays. His works explored the themes of relationships and alienation and were often critical of society. Strindberg won recognition with *The Red Room* (1879) and went on to write several masterpieces, including the psychological drama

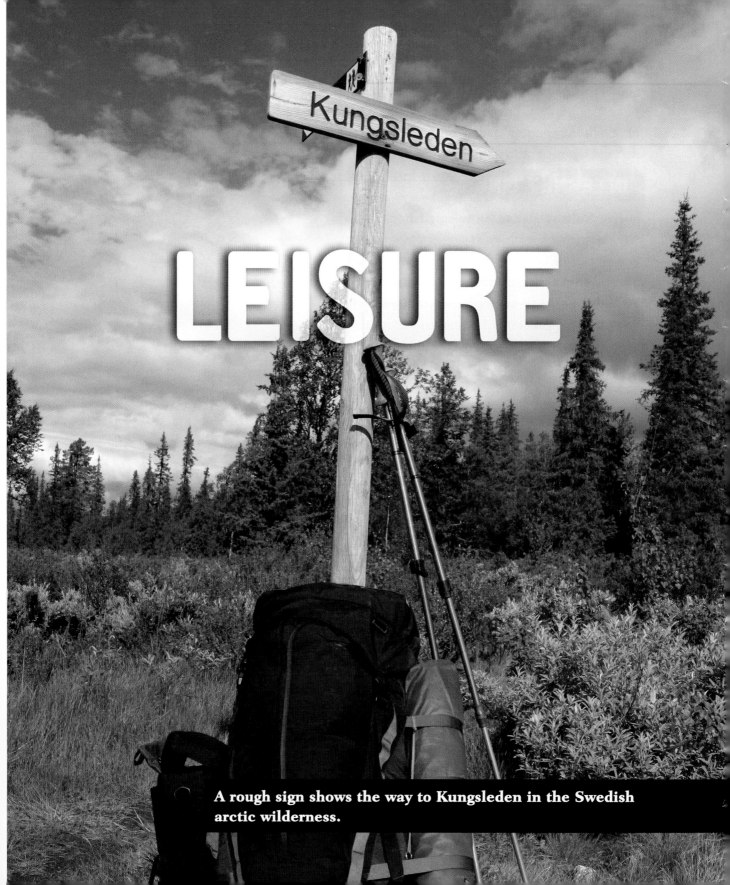

LEISURE

A rough sign shows the way to Kungsleden in the Swedish arctic wilderness.

11

WHEN SUMMER IS AS SHORT AS it is in Sweden, people naturally want to make the most of it. Sure enough, most workers enjoy six to ten weeks of vacation a year, and for most people, July is the best time for it. Summer kicks off in a big way at the end of June with Midsummer, one of the most important celebrations of the year.

Sweden is a nation of sports lovers. More than one-third of Swedes age sixteen to eighty-four are members of at least one athletic organization, and nearly half of seven- to nineteen-year-olds compete in sports.

A boy jumps in a lake in summer.

Most leisure activities take place outdoors, as Swedes enjoy being close to nature and escaping city life as often as they can. Outdoor leisure pursuits enable Swedes to combine two great interests: being with the family and enjoying the countryside. Playing some kind of sport is also a popular pastime, for fun and fitness. Sports, whether competitive or friendly, are always taken seriously.

Anders Soedergren of Sweden leads a pack in the men's 50-km cross-country ski race during 2014 Winter Olympics in Sochi, Russia.

SPORTS

There was a time when Sweden dominated the world of pro tennis. In 1988, Swedish tennis stars Stefan Edberg and Mats Wilander, between them, won all four of the major Opens. For about a decade in the 1970s and '80s, the legendary Björn Borg proved to be one of the greatest tennis players of all time. These superstars helped make tennis a Swedish passion. Though the twenty-first century hasn't seen a new Swedish tennis player of the likes of those earlier champs, the sport is still important.

Ice hockey and association football (soccer) are the national spectator sports. The Swedish Hockey League (SHL), the highest level of men's hockey in Sweden, attracted 1,974,388 spectators in the 2013—14 season, the highest overall attendance in Swedish sports. In the 2014—2015 season, the league expanded to include fourteen teams.

The Swedish men's national hockey team, nicknamed *Tre Kronor* ("Three Crowns"), is one of the top five ice hockey teams in the world. In 2013, it ranked number one. Swedes have also distinguished themselves in the prestigious Canada Cup ice hockey competition, and won gold at the 1994 and 2006 Winter Olympics. Sweden also has a top women's national hockey team, nicknamed *Damkronorna* ("Lady Crowns"). They finished fourth in the 2014 Olympics and that same year, ranked sixth in the world.

Swedes also dominate in other winter sports. In the 2014 Olympic Games in Sochi, Russia, both the women's and men's cross country skiing teams took gold medals. Of those skiers, Charlotte Kalla emerged as one of Sweden's most popular women athletes.

In soccer, Zlatan Ibrahimovic has been Sweden's top scorer and is an immensely popular star, as is Lotta Schelin of the women's soccer team. In golf, another popular sport, Sweden's Annika Sörenstam became a huge name from 1995 to 2008, winning ninety international tournaments.

MASS SPORTS

Swedes enjoy doing things together, and this is especially true in sports. Mass races, where participants number in the thousands, are a very old tradition in Sweden. Often, mass events take place over long distances, testing participants' endurance. Several mass sports events attract many people throughout the year.

Some 15,800 skiers prepare to start the 88th Vasaloppet cross-country ski marathon in Mora on March 4, 2012.

The most famous mass event is the *Vasaloppet* ("Vasa Race"), where more than 12,000 cross-country skiers compete in a 56-mile (90-km) race from the village of Sälen to the village of Mora in the county of Dalarna. Held on the first Sunday every March, the Vasa Race commemorates the escape of Gustav Vasa from the 1520 Bloodbath of Stockholm. The Vasa is the oldest, longest, and biggest (having most participants) cross-country ski marathon in the world.

Another mass event is the O-ringen, a five-day orienteering race that attracts as many as 20,000 people who run cross-country using a compass and a map for direction.

Long distance hikers take a breather during an autumn trek.

Church boat races are held every year on Lake Mora as part of the midsummer festival. The race originates from the boat trips people once had to take across the lake from their homes to get to church on the other side. In the races today, the boats carry twenty rowers and passengers who race across the lake dressed in their best clothes.

Other popular events are the Lidingö Race for joggers, the Vansbro Swim, and the Vättern Circuit, a two-day bicycle race along Lake Vättern.

LEARNING ABOUT NATURE

Most recreational activities in Sweden take advantage of the fresh air and rich natural landscape. As more than half of Sweden's land area is wooded, there are plenty of opportunities for nature treks and learning firsthand about the country's flora and fauna.

School groups often take field trips, which supplement classroom learning. Many of these trips teach students about ecology and the natural environment.

Walking is a popular pastime, and families often go off on long treks together during the warmer months. These walks usually turn into nature studies as children are taught to identify different types of wildflowers, trees, and birds. One may spot an elk, a bear, or even a lynx.

There is a network of marked trails all over Sweden. Many of these are dotted with rest stations that allow trekkers to spend the night in some comfort. The most well-known trail is the Kungsleden, or Royal Route, in the north; it is more than 300 miles (483 km) long.

In the winter, cross-country skiing replaces walking. This form of skiing is almost second nature to Swedes, although many young people prefer the thrill of downhill skiing.

Summer houses dot the Swedish shoreline.

IT'S SUMMERTIME!

Summer in Sweden is short and active. From the very start of the season, Swedes pack their vacation bags, get into cars, buses, or trains, and head out to the countryside or onto the beaches.

Two girls show off some of the wild mushrooms they gathered in the woods.

Most families either own a summer house in the countryside or have access to one, where they spend a good part of their summer vacation. Typically, many vacation days are spent picking different types of wild berries, such as strawberries, raspberries, and blueberries. *Lingon* (LING-gon), or cowberry, as well as rose hips and blackberries are the choice of the autumn season. Lingon grows all over the country, while another popular berry, the yellow, raspberry-shaped *hjorton* (YOO-tron), or cloudberry, is found in the north.

The end of the summer is also the time for picking mushrooms. Walks in the woods turn into mushroom-hunting expeditions, and both young and old search the undergrowth for different types of edible mushrooms, such as chanterelles, cepes, and ringed boletuses.

Swedes take berry- and mushroom-picking so seriously that they organize trips to the woods during the picking season. They also attend classes to learn about different kinds of fungi, especially to differentiate the edible species from the inedible ones.

FISHING

Fishing is perhaps the favorite noncompetitive sport of Swedes. With thousands of lakes and rivers, home to a variety of fish, such as salmon, perch, and pike, it is not surprising that over one million people in Sweden indulge in this pastime. And fishing doesn't end when the lakes freeze over. That's the time for ice fishing, in which fishermen drill holes in thick lake ice and dangle bait into the water below. In one form of ice fishing, *kikmete*, or "bait watching," the fishers lie down on reindeer skins to peer into the hole to watch their bait. This way they can watch as a fish comes up and takes the bait.

A little girl waits patiently by an ice-fishing hole on a frozen lake in Varmland.

INTERNET LINKS

sweden.se/culture/20-swedish-superstars-in-sports
"Twenty Swedish Superstars in Sports" is a feature of the Sweden.se site.

www.oringen.se/english/orteren/skane2014.652_en.html
In 2014, the O-ringen celebrated its 50th anniversary.

sweden.se/nature/10-reasons-to-spend-winter-in-sweden
"Ten Reasons to Spend Winter in Sweden" lists fun winter activities.

FESTIVALS

A little girl dresses as a traditional Easter witch (or Easter hag) and carries willow branches decorated with feathers.

12

S WEDISH HOLIDAYS ARE MOSTLY happy affairs tied to the changing seasons and Christian saint days. Although many modern Swedes are quite secular in their thinking, religious holidays still form a major part of the festive calendar, and religious traditions continue. All special days—even the somber occasions—are celebrated in uniquely Swedish ways, usually with plenty of good food, music, dancing, drinking, and general merriment.

EASTER

Swedes solemnly observe Easter week, which begins with Palm Sunday. There are no palm processions as in Roman Catholic countries, partly because palms do not grow in Sweden's cold climate. Instead, people place budding varieties of willow branches in vases of water at home or at the office, and the branches sprout leaves by the time Palm Sunday arrives. In some parts of the country, these branches are called palms.

A lighter side of Easter celebrations is in dressing children as "Easter hags" on Maundy Thursday, the eve of Good Friday. The Easter hags visit neighbors and hand out decorated cards, hoping for sweets or a coin in

For many Swedes, it wouldn't be Christmas Eve without watching Donald Duck (*Kalle Anka*) in an old Disney cartoon special from 1958. (In Sweden, Donald Duck is far more popular than Mickey Mouse.) For unexplained reasons, watching this particular show at 3:00 in the afternoon of Christmas Eve has become a nostalgic Swedish tradition.

A smiling girl poses by a spring bonfire.

return. In western Sweden, this Easter card or letter is often secretly slipped into the mailbox or under the door. Easter eggs are traditionally eaten the evening before Easter Sunday.

In the western provinces, villages make huge bonfires, with many competing to see who has the biggest bonfire. Fireworks are also let off as part of the festivities. These customs stem from the old superstitious belief that witches came out especially during Easter week, flying off on their broomsticks on Maundy Thursday to meet the devil and flying back the following Saturday. People in those times lit bonfires, shot their firearms into the sky, and painted crosses on their doors, to protect themselves against the witches' black magic.

THE FEAST OF VALBORG

The Feast of Valborg, also known as Walpurgis Night, is a feast not of food but of song. It is the evening when everyone welcomes spring; it is celebrated on April 30 every year, although spring is still weeks away in the north.

One of the most colorful celebrations of the Feast of Valborg is held at Uppsala University, where students gather in the thousands all afternoon. At exactly 3 p.m., they all put on white caps to mark the change in seasons, and they sing traditional songs about spring. This is followed by parties that last until dawn the next day—May Day.

Meanwhile, people elsewhere gather around community bonfires to deliver or hear speeches and to sing a welcome to the return of light. The bonfires have other purposes besides getting rid of trash and witches—they are also supposed to scare away wild animals. Scaring away wild animals is especially important, because cattle are traditionally brought out to pasture on May 1.

May Day sees the start of springtime activities such as picnics and outdoor games. Since it is also Labor Day, it is marked by parades and speeches by labor and political leaders.

LET'S CELEBRATE!

NATIONAL DAY Like most countries, Sweden sets aside a day to commemorate its nationhood. National Day falls on June 6 and is celebrated in schools and most towns with parades, brass bands, and speeches. The king also presents flags to associations and organizations. National Day is a normal working day in Sweden and the celebrations are relatively quiet compared to those in other countries.

A student color guard conducts a flag ceremony on National Day, June 6, 2014, in Ronneby.

HALLOWEEN This ancient Celtic holiday is a new arrival in Sweden, where people only began celebrating it in the 1990s. Curiously, the Swedish version of trick-or-treat occurs at Easter time, with its Easter hag tradition. Nevertheless, the foreign import of Halloween is now celebrated mostly by children and young people, who enjoy the ghostly traditions as a welcome diversion as the year grows dark. The new interest in Halloween has led to an increase in pumpkin growing on the Swedish island of Öland in the southern Baltic Sea.

NEW YEAR'S EVE After the Christmas festivities, New Year's Eve is often a quiet affair. Many Swedes spend New Year's Eve quietly at home with family or friends. Others may set off fireworks in the streets.

MIDSUMMER

Living in such a northern country, Swedes understandably love summer. Midsummer is a major festival, traditionally celebrated on June 23, and now celebrated on the Friday closest to June 23. This is the time when summer days are the longest, and the midnight sun shines all day and night.

The word midsummer *is used throughout northern Europe to mark the beginning—not the middle—of summer. One of William Shakespeare's most beloved plays, "A Midsummer Night's Dream," which he wrote between 1590 and 1596, reflects this usage. The term comes from centuries past, when the old Anglo-Saxon and Icelandic calendars had only two seasons, summer and winter. According to these calendars, summer would have begun on the spring equinox in March and "Midsummer's Day" would have fallen around the time of the June solstice.*

On this day, people decorate homes, cars, churches, and other public places with garlands of flowers and leafy branches. Then they gather around a maypole called majstång *("MAH-EE-stohng") to dress it with flowers and leaves. They erect the tall, floral-decked cross in the village square or a playground, and young and old alike dance and sing around the decorated maypole. Some places, such as Dalarna in central Sweden, are famous for their midsummer festivities and attract hordes of tourists.*

There are several superstitions attached to the midsummer festival. The dew that night holds special properties and, if collected, can be used to cure illnesses. Certain plants are collected for the same purpose. Young people pick a bouquet of seven types of flowers and place them under their pillow, so they will dream of their future spouse. The future can also be seen by eating "dream herring" and "dream porridge" with plenty of salt in it.

LUCIA DAY AND CHRISTMAS

The most eagerly anticipated festival of the year is Christmas, which lasts from early December to mid-January. The Advent season begins in early December, when people attend special church services. Wreaths, lights, and Christmas trees are put up along streets and in town squares on the first Sunday of December.

At home, families begin the countdown to Christmas by lighting a candle on each of the four Sundays leading up to Christmas. Children have an Advent calendar—cards with date "windows" to be opened each day until Christmas Day.

Lucia Day is celebrated in homes, schools, and communities on December 13 in commemoration of St. Lucia of Syracuse. At home, Lucia Day begins before dawn with a daughter of the family dressing up as St. Lucia, in a long white gown and a crown of candles. She awakens her family with a tray of coffee, saffron buns, and ginger snaps for breakfast.

Lucia pageants are performed at schools, clubs, and community gatherings. A St. Lucia, or "queen of light," is chosen from among the young girls. She leads a procession of attendants dressed in white gowns—handmaidens with glitter in their hair and star boys wearing tall, conical hats and carrying a star on a stake. The children sing traditional carols and songs.

Christmas Eve is the most festive day of the season. People start the day by decorating the Christmas tree with typical Swedish ornaments: the

Swedish kindergarten children celebrate Lucia Day. Saint Lucia lived in Syracuse, Sicily, and died a martyr's death in the year 304. Her feast day has become associated with light in the darkest time of the year.

January 1	New Year's Day
March/April	Easter week
April 30	Feast of Valborg
May 1	May (Labor) Day
May/June	Ascension Day
June	Pentecost
June 6	National Day
June 23	Midsummer
November	All Saints' Day
November 11	St. Martin's Day
December	Advent
December 13	Lucia Day
December 25	Christmas Day
December 26	St. Stephen's Day

Christmas gnome (*jultomte*), Noel goat (*julbok*), straw figurines, and tiny Swedish flags, along with ginger cookies in different shapes. At about 3 p.m., the feasting begins with a traditional *smörgåsbord* ("SMOER-gos-bord") and continues into the evening. After a lavish meal, the children wait for the Christmas gnome, called *tomte* ("TOM-teh"), a Swedish version of Santa Claus. He is expected to appear with presents. It is customary for an adult disguised as the tomte to visit the children with gifts. The children get very excited, because by tradition, they have to invite him in for a meal of rice porridge, his favorite food.

Church services are held early on Christmas morning, and the rest of the day is spent quietly with the family. Some families continue the merrymaking up to Twelfth Night, or Epiphany, on January 6. The Christmas season ends on Knut's Day on January 13, when the Christmas tree is taken down. Children and their friends take down the tree, have a party, and eat up the edible decorations.

NAMNSDAG

Namnsdag, or Name Day, is almost as important as one's birthday in Sweden. Almost every day of the year is given a name. For example, July 23 is Emma day, and December 11 is Daniel day. In old times, children were given the name of the day they were born on. Everyone with a Swedish name has a day for his or her name and receives greeting cards or flowers from family and friends.

"Name Day, A Day of Celebration" (1902) is a painting by the Swedish artist **Fanny Brate**. It is her most famous work.

INTERNET LINKS

www.nytimes.com/2013/05/12/travel/a-midsummer-days-dream-in-sweden.html?_r=0
This *New York Times* article is a wonderful, long, first-person description of a Midsummer celebration in the south of Sweden.

www.slate.com/articles/arts/culturebox/2009/12/nordic_quack.html
Slate's "Nordic Quack" examines the Swedish custom of watching A Disney cartoon special on Christmas Eve.

sweden.se/collection/celebrating-the-swedish-way
"Celebrating the Swedish Way" offers thirteen articles about Swedish holidays and festivities.

en.wikipedia.org/wiki/Swedish_name_day_list_of_2001
"Swedish name day list of 2001" is a calendar of the most recently-updated name day list, as determined by the Swedish Academy.

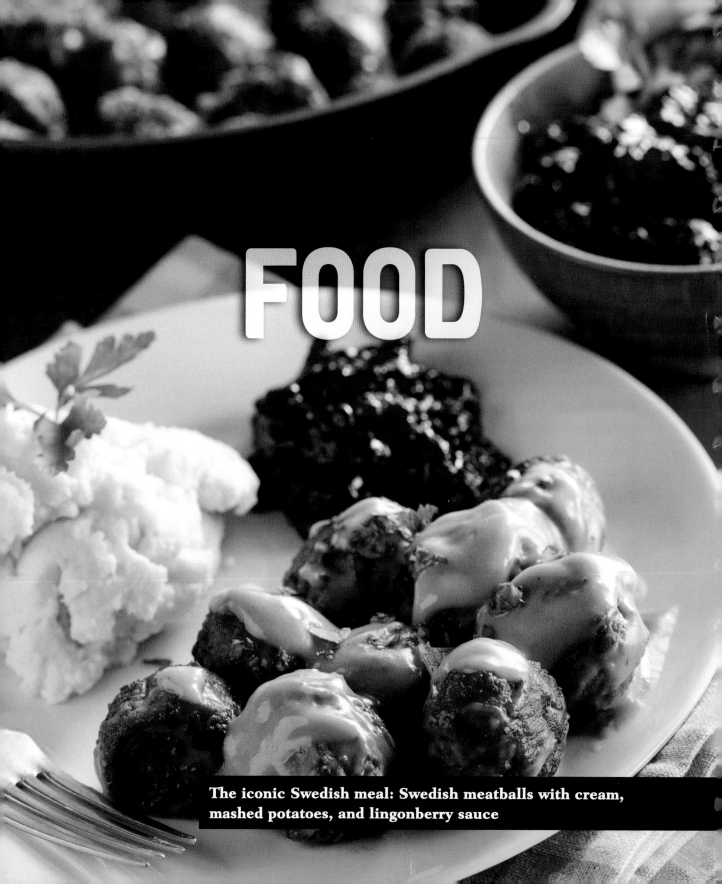

FOOD

The iconic Swedish meal: Swedish meatballs with cream, mashed potatoes, and lingonberry sauce

LONG BEFORE IKEA MADE SWEDISH meatballs a popular cafeteria offering at their many stores around the world, the cream-sauced meatballs were a culinary hit in the United States. Accompanied by boiled potatoes and the mandatory lingonberry sauce—hard to find in the U.S.—the meatballs were perhaps the only Swedish dish most Americans could name.

Wild lingonberries, produced by low, evergreen shrubs, grow abundantly in Sweden

13

In 2008, Sweden's Minister for Rural Affairs, Eskil Erlandsson, introduced a plan to promote Sweden as "The New Culinary Nation." The goal is to establish Swedish food as a major international cuisine based on its health benefits, cleanliness (Sweden is salmonella-free), renowned chefs, and environmentally sustainable production practices.

A Swedish retiree enjoys a cup of coffee at a coffee shop.

Swedish cookery reflects the country's cold climate, short growing season and abundance of coastline. Pickled, cured, and salted fish—particularly salmon and herring—is a mainstay of the diet, along with pork, potatoes, cheese, and bread. Pork and beef, the favorite meats, are often made into sausages, and one can find reindeer and moose meat on some dinner tables, particularly in Norrland.

Fresh vegetables play a minor role, a result of the short growing season, though root vegetables such as turnips and beets are more common. Fresh berries add a bright note, and lingonberries are ubiquitous. Swedes use lingonberry sauce the way other people use catsup, salsa, or hot sauce; it goes with everything.

By some standards, Swedish food is bland, as spices are used lightly, but fresh herbs such as dill are highly favored. Spices that Swedish cooks often use in both sweet and savory foods include allspice, nutmeg, cardamom, and saffron. Swedes love their sweets, and the cuisine is rich with pastries, pies, and cookies.

As a drink, milk is not just for children. Most Swedes drink several glasses of it a day. Swedes are also great coffee drinkers, and the coffee break, called *fika*, is considered a national institution.

MEALTIMES

Breakfast is usually a meal of cereal, bread, butter, and cheese, with coffee, tea, *filmjölk*, a fermented milk product similar to buttermilk or kefir, or yogurt. The main meal of the day, called middag (MID-dahg), is traditionally served at 4 p.m., followed by a supper of coffee and cakes or a cold buffet after 8 p.m. However, these traditional mealtimes are not practical for working people, who instead have a light lunch at 12:30 p.m. A smörgås (SMOER-gos), or an open-faced sandwich, is the most popular lunchtime food and a well-

The smörgås, *or open-faced sandwich, is a Scandinavian specialty. The concept of open sandwiches dates back to the 1400s when thick slabs of bread were used as plates. In a similar way, a Swedish* smörgås *is a beautifully composed meal on top of a piece or two of buttered bread. The bread is usually a whole-grain rye or a thinly sliced brown bread.*

The topping may consist of herring, smoked salmon, shrimp, or steak; sliced hard boiled eggs; thinly sliced cucumber, tomato, and/or pickled beets; and some sprigs of dill or parsley. An herbed mayonnaise or creme fraiche accompanies the dish. The shrimp sandwich (räksmörgås) *is perhaps the most elegant option, served with butter lettuce, lemon wedges, and even a bit of fish roe.*

known example of Swedish cuisine. People usually have dinner after coming home from the office. This includes a main dish of meat or fish with potatoes, and cheese or fruit.

Swedish appreciation for international foods is increasing as immigrants, restaurants, and the Internet bring new ideas to the culture.

TABLE MANNERS

Swedes like things well-ordered. This is true even in the social sphere, where rules of behavior are kept. These rules apply at formal dinners as well as casual meals. For example, Swedes are always punctual; it is considered bad manners to be late. Many arrive early and wait to present themselves at the door at the appointed time. It is customary to bring a gift, perhaps a box of chocolates or even a bouquet of flowers, for the hostess.

To start the meal, the host gives a short speech and then raises his glass for the first *skål* (skohl), or toast, to welcome his guests. The guests are expected to reply with the word skål and then establish eye contact with fellow guests, especially those sitting across from or closest to them. Eye contact is reestablished after a sip is taken.

At a formal dinner, guests are not supposed to drink their wine unless in a skål. They either have to offer a toast or wait to be toasted. At an informal meal, the host will usually announce that "drinking is free," which means that guests are allowed to drink without having to skål one another. A popular story explains the origin of this custom from the time of the Vikings. They trusted no one and thus made toasts while keeping an eye out for any unpleasant surprises (like a stab in the heart).

Toward the end of the meal, the guest on the left of the hostess is expected to give a short speech of thanks on behalf of the others. Children are taught at an early age to thank their hostess by saying "*Tack förmaten*," (tahk fur MAH-tehn), meaning "Thank you for the food." Guests are expected to give a phone call or send a note the next day to thank the hostess for her hospitality.

TRADITIONAL COOKING METHODS

A lot of Swedish food is still prepared using traditional methods. A good example is the preparation of fish, a staple in the diet.

In the old days, the irregular supply of fish and the difficulty of fishing during the winter in the frozen north gave rise to different methods of preserving fish. It is not surprising to still find a number of dishes that include salted, dried, or smoked fish.

Gravad lax (GRAH-vahd lax), or marinated salmon, is one of the most well-known Swedish dishes. The method of marinating, or *gravning* (GRAHV-ning), is one of the oldest curing methods. Gravning comes from the word *begrava* (beh-GRAH-vah), which means bury. The old method was to bury the fish after salting it lightly to preserve it, because salt was an expensive commodity. This method of preparation also gave rise to fermentation, another old Swedish preservation method.

Fish is no longer buried or fermented to marinate. The fish is simply rubbed with salt, sugar, and herbs and left to cure for a day or two in the refrigerator.

Meat was also dried and salted in the old days. *Spicken* (SPICK-kehn), another word with ancient roots, referred to the method of stretching out meat or fish on wooden sticks to dry in the sun, after which it would be salted. Today, meats are still sun-dried and salted, but fish is just salted.

One area where tradition prevails is in the baking of *knäckebröd* (ker-NECK-keh-brod), or crispbread, sometimes called hard bread. Most varieties of this unleavened, wholemeal rye bread are machine-made, although some are baked in old-fashioned wooden stoves in certain areas such as Dalarna. This large, thin, round bread had a hole in its center, through which a pole would be threaded and hung above the family's wooden stove. This was the traditional method of storing crispbread.

Smoked whitefish like these are a favorite dish in Sweden.

A variety of fish dishes are served at a buffet.

Originally, crispbread was coarse in texture, dry, and durable due to the high temperature at which it was baked. Today, however, it is possible to find a variety of crispbreads with different textures and hardness.

THE SMÖRGÅSBORD

The best example of Sweden's food heritage is found in the *smörgåsbord*, which means "open sandwich table." The smörgåsbord is a buffet-style meal of cold and hot dishes where diners help themselves to the great variety of excellent Swedish cuisine.

The practice of laying out different dishes on the table is said to have started in the sixteenth century. *Smörgås-bord* is said to be descended from the *brännvin* (BRAN-vin) table, where the first course of a banquet was laid on a separate table. Guests stood for this course of brännvin (vodka made from corn or potatoes), herring, anchovies, bread, and strong cheese. They would then be seated for the main meal.

Over the centuries, more dishes were added to the first course until its peak in the nineteenth century, when it began to be served in homes and restaurants. Today, the smörgåsbord is no longer the first course but the whole meal for Swedes. Since they no longer have the time to prepare the same enormous amount and variety of food, they offer scaled-down versions when entertaining at home. Nevertheless, on special occasions and especially at Christmas, they do still celebrate with a laden table that recalls their heritage.

In a traditional smörgåsbord, the table is piled with as many as forty dishes, all laid out together. However, to truly appreciate the meal, diners have the smörgåsbord in five courses. The general rule is to serve fish dishes first, then cold meats and salads, then hot dishes, and finally desserts. Bread and butter are served throughout the first four courses.

In the first course, people sample a variety of herrings prepared in different ways (salted, pickled, marinated; in cream sauce, dill, sherry), and strong, hard cheeses, accompanied by crispbread. The second course offers fish such as mackerel and cod, with salmon being the highlight.

Cold meats make up the third course; this includes delicacies such as dried leg of mutton and smoked reindeer and is accompanied by salads and pickled vegetables. In the fourth course, hot dishes are served, including meatballs, a favorite of Swedish children, and Jansson's Temptation, a baked dish of potatoes and anchovies.

The fifth course completes the meal with desserts: creamy cakes, Swedish apple pies, and fresh fruit.

Although smörgåsbord meals are found all over Sweden, Skåne province is especially famous for its smörgåsbord.

The anglicized word *smorgasbord* has entered the English language and tends to be used for any buffet-style meal featuring a variety of dishes.

For many Swedish adults, a festive occasion calls for aquavit.

SNAPS

No smörgåsbord is complete without *snaps* (snahps), or aquavit, drunk by the glassful. Snaps glasses are relatively small, but even a small quantity packs a powerful punch. Snaps is made from potatoes or barley and varies a great deal in flavor. Different types of herbs and spices, such as caraway seeds, cumin, and dill, are used in the flavoring. There are at least twenty flavored snaps to choose from.

The importance of snaps in Swedish drinking tradition is found in the drinking ritual. There is no ritual in the drinking of beer, which is also drunk with the smörgåsbord. But for snaps, it is very important to raise glasses for a mutual toast before drinking, after which either the skål rule applies or guests are allowed to drink at their liberty. According to an old tradition, husbands are expected to skål their wives. If they forget, their wives can demand a pair of hosiery as compensation.

What Swedes really enjoy most is a song before gulping down the snaps. These traditional drinking songs are sung by everyone and end almost in a

Traditional S-shaped saffron buns are a sweet treat.

shout. There are countless songs, some with witty lyrics and full of puns. Different occasions call for different songs, although they can be sung in any season.

FESTIVE FOODS

The most important date in the Swedish calendar is Christmas. Early in December, the smell of spicy Christmas food being baked wafts through the air. Even those who rarely bake try their hand at turning out gingersnaps, saffron buns, and *drömmar*, a crisp cookie.

On Lucia Day, December 13, people in the office gather in their coffee corners, sipping spiced, mulled wine and eating ginger snaps and saffron buns. The wine is a mixture of red wine and snaps, spiced with cinnamon, cloves, and cardamom. This spicy, sweet mix is served piping hot with raisins and almonds. Gingersnaps are thin, crisp, spice cookies that are eaten year round and especially during Christmas.

Children have their share of the festive goodies, except the hot wine; they enjoy hot chocolate instead.

The smörgåsbord eaten on the afternoon of Christmas Eve presents a slightly different spread from that eaten during the rest of the year. It has sweet-sour red cabbage, mustard-glazed baked ham, sausages, and pickled pigs' feet. Certain dishes commemorate old times. For example, "Dip in the Pot" recalls the time when poor farm hands were invited to dip their bread in the broth where ham and other meats had been boiled. That was the closest they got to tasting the ham. Today, a special herb-flavored bread is dipped in this tasty broth.

Another winter dish is *lutfisk* (LOOT-fisk), a salted and dried codfish soaked in lye from December 9 so that it is ready on Christmas Day.

Young children in Sweden leave a bowl of rice porridge for the Christmas tomte to eat when he comes to visit them. This thick rice pudding type of porridge is eaten as a dessert on Christmas Eve. Rice is boiled with milk and served with sugar and cinnamon. Sometimes a single almond is added, and tradition says that a single person who gets the almond in his or her portion will be married within the year.

INTERNET LINKS

www.tryswedish.com/en
"Try Swedish!" is the website of "The New Culinary Nation" and offers in-depth stories and beautiful photos about the role of food in Sweden's culture.

sweden.se/culture/10-things-to-know-about-swedish-food
"10 Things to Know About Swedish Food" is part of the Sweden.se site and gives a lively overview of the subject.

www.swedishfood.com
SwedishFood.com is "dedicated to bringing tried and tasted Swedish recipes to English speakers around the world."

DRÖMMAR: SWEDISH DREAM COOKIES

These classic cookies smell horrible when they are cooking, but they are dreamy once they are finished. That's because of the baker's ammonia, an essential ingredient which produces the cookie's special texture. This old-fashioned ingredient can be hard to find, however, so twice the amount of baking powder can be substituted, but the results will not be quite the same.

1 stick unsalted butter, softened
1 ¼ cups sugar
1 tsp vanilla extract
⅓ cup vegetable oil
1 tsp baker's ammonia, also called hornsalt or powdered ammonium carbonate (or 2 tsp baking powder)
1 ⅔ cups all-purpose flour

Preheat oven to 300 degrees F. Line baking sheet with parchment paper or Silpat mats.

In the bowl of a mixer, beat together the butter, sugar, and vanilla until light and fluffy. Slowly add the oil with the mixer on low speed. Add in the baker's ammonia and flour and beat until combined. The dough will be on the drier side. Form 1-inch balls and place 2 inches apart on the baking sheet.

Bake for about 15—20 minutes, or until cookies have just begun to set. Let cookies cool on baking sheet for 5 minutes and then transfer cookies to a wire cooling rack and let cool completely.

KROPPKAKOR (SWEDISH POTATO DUMPLINGS)

These are also often made with a mushroom-onion filling. Leftovers are good sliced in half and fried in butter.

(4—6 servings)

10 medium-sized potatoes
2—3 egg yolks
1 ¼ cup flour
1 tsp salt
1 onion, finely chopped
8 oz ground pork or chopped bacon
1 tsp allspice
dash nutmeg

Peel and boil the potatoes. Mash them and mix with the egg yolks and salt. Let the purée cool, then mix in the flour. Knead the dough thoroughly and shape into a long roll. Fry the pork or bacon with the onion and mix with the allspice. Cut the potato roll into inch-thick slices, make a depression in the center of each slice and fill it with the pork mixture. Flatten each dumpling so the pork mixture is in the middle and roll into a smooth, even ball. Boil the dumplings slowly in a pot of lightly salted water without a lid for 5—6 minutes after the dumplings rise to the surface. Serve with lingonberry jam, cream, and melted butter. The dumplings can also be cut in half and fried in butter.

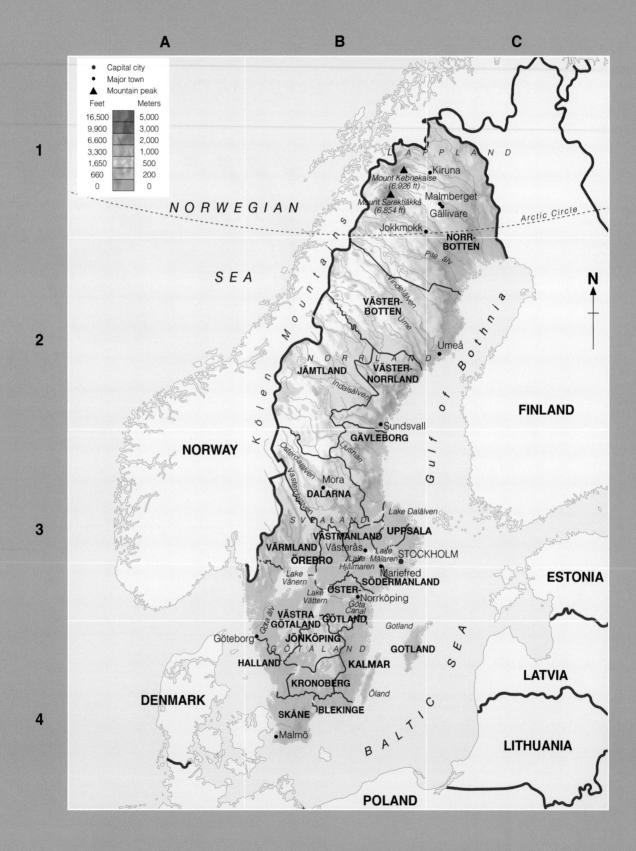

A **B** **C**

- Capital city
- Major town
▲ Mountain peak

Feet	Meters
16,500	5,000
9,900	3,000
6,600	2,000
3,300	1,000
1,650	500
660	200
0	0

1

L A P P L A N D

▲ Mount Kebnekaise
(6,926 ft) • Kiruna

• Malmberget
Mount Sarektjåkkå ▲ • Gällivare
(6,854 ft)

Arctic Circle

• Jokkmokk **NORR-
BOTTEN**

Pite älv

N O R W E G I A N

Vindelälven

**VÄSTER-
BOTTEN**

Ume

2

S E A

N O R R L A N D

JÄMTLAND **VÄSTER-
NORRLAND**

Indalsälven

G u l f   o f   B o t h n i a

• Umeå

FINLAND

N

NORWAY

• Sundsvall
GÄVLEBORG

Ljusnan

Österdalälven

• Mora
DALARNA

Västerdalälven

S V E A L A N D

Lake Dalälven

3

VÄSTMANLAND **UPPSALA**

VÄRMLAND Västerås • *Lake
Mälaren* • STOCKHOLM
ÖREBRO *Lake
Hjälmaren* • Mariefred

*Lake
Vänern* **SÖDERMANLAND**

*Lake
Vättern* **ÖSTER-** • Norrköping

ESTONIA

*Göta
Canal*

**VÄSTRA
GÖTALAND** **GÖTLAND**

Göta älv *Gotland*

Göteborg • **JÖNKÖPING**

G Ö T A L A N D

HALLAND **GOTLAND**

KALMAR

LATVIA

KRONOBERG

Öland

DENMARK

4

SKÅNE **BLEKINGE**

B A L T I C   S E A

LITHUANIA

• Malmö

POLAND

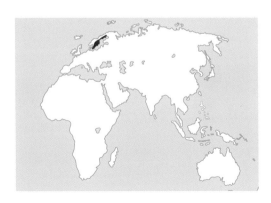

ECONOMIC SWEDEN

Services

 Airport

 Port

Manufacturing

 Vehicles

Natural Resources

 Crystal

 Hydroelectricity

 Iron and Steel

 Nuclear Reactor

 Timber

Farming

 Reindeer

 Vegetables

 Wheat

ABOUT THE ECONOMY

OVERVIEW

Sweden's mixed system of high-tech capitalism and generous welfare benefits, modern distribution and communications systems, and highly skilled labor force all contribute to a robust economy. Nevertheless, it is subject to declines linked to weakness in the European Union, its main export market.

DOMESTIC PRODUCT (GDP)

$393.8 billion (2013)
Per capita: $40,900 (2013)

NATURAL RESOURCES

Metals (zinc, iron ore, lead, copper, silver), timber, uranium, hydropower

GDP SECTORS

Agriculture 2 percent, industry 31.3 percent, services 66.8 percent (2013)

LAND USE

Arable land 5.8 percent, permanent pastures .02 percent, other 94.18 percent

CURRENCY

Swedish krona (SEK)
1 krona = 100 öre
USD 1 = SEK 6.8798 (August 2014)
Notes: 20, 50, 100, 500, 1000 kroner
Coins: 50 öre; 1, 5, 10 kroner

INFLATION RATE

0 percent (2014)
Labor force
5.107 million

LABOR DISTRIBUTION

Agriculture 2 percent, industry 24 percent, services 74 percent

UNEMPLOYMENT RATE

8.2 percent (2014)

AGRICULTURAL PRODUCTS

Grain, sugar beets, potatoes, meat, milk

INDUSTRIAL PRODUCTS

Iron and steel, armaments, electronics, wood pulp and paper, processed foods, motor vehicles

MAJOR TRADE PARTNERS

European Union (Germany, United Kingdom, Denmark, Finland, France), United States, Norway

TOTAL EXPORTS

$181.5 billion (2013)

TOTAL IMPORTS

$158 billion (2013)

PORTS AND HARBORS

Gävle, Göteborg, Halmstad, Hälsingborg, Helsingborg, Kalmar, Karlshamn, Malmö, Solvesborg, Stockholm, Sundsvall

AIRPORTS

231 total; 149 with paved runways (2013)

CULTURAL SWEDEN

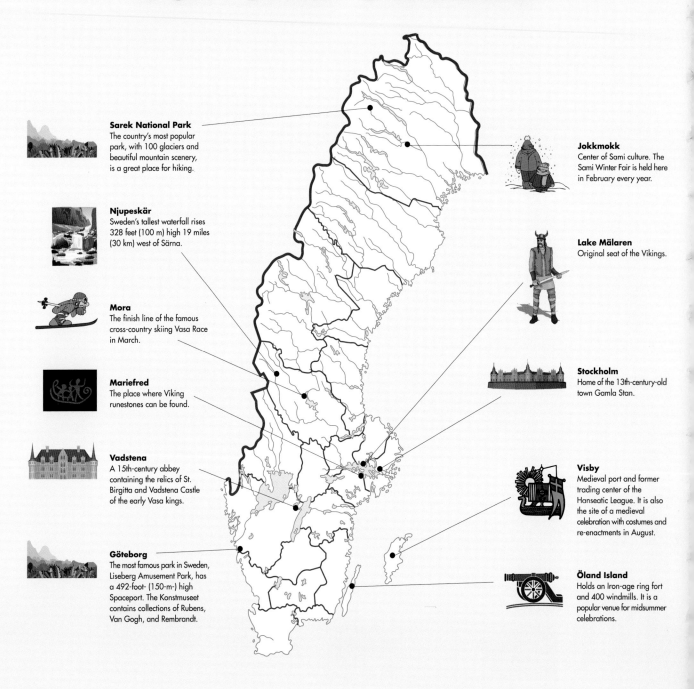

Sarek National Park
The country's most popular park, with 100 glaciers and beautiful mountain scenery, is a great place for hiking.

Njupeskär
Sweden's tallest waterfall rises 328 feet (100 m) high 19 miles (30 km) west of Särna.

Mora
The finish line of the famous cross-country skiing Vasa Race in March.

Mariefred
The place where Viking runestones can be found.

Vadstena
A 15th-century abbey containing the relics of St. Birgitta and Vadstena Castle of the early Vasa kings.

Göteborg
The most famous park in Sweden, Liseberg Amusement Park, has a 492-foot- (150-m-) high Spaceport. The Konstmuseet contains collections of Rubens, Van Gogh, and Rembrandt.

Jokkmokk
Center of Sami culture. The Sami Winter Fair is held here in February every year.

Lake Mälaren
Original seat of the Vikings.

Stockholm
Home of the 13th-century-old town Gamla Stan.

Visby
Medieval port and former trading center of the Hanseatic League. It is also the site of a medieval celebration with costumes and re-enactments in August.

Öland Island
Holds an Iron-age ring fort and 400 windmills. It is a popular venue for midsummer celebrations.

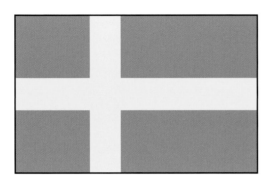

OFFICIAL NAME
Kingdom of Sweden

NATIONAL FLAG
Blue background with a yellow cross that extends to the edges; the vertical axis of the cross is nearer the hoist.

NATIONAL ANTHEM
Du gamla, du fria (Thou ancient, thou free). Words by R. Dybeck set to folk music.

CAPITAL
Stockholm

ADMINISTRATIVE DIVISIONS (COUNTIES)
Blekinge, Dalarna, Gävleborg, Gotland, Halland, Jämtland, Jönköping, Kalmar, Kronoberg, Norrbotten, Örebro, Östergötland, Skåne, Södermanland, Stockholm, Uppsala, Värmland, Västerbotten, Västernorrland, Västmanland, Västra Götaland

POPULATION
9,723,809 (2014)

POPULATION GROWTH RATE
0.79 percent (2014)

AGE STRUCTURE
14 years and below: 17 percent; 15 to 64 years: 62.5 percent; 65 years and over: 20.5 percent (2014)

LIFE EXPECTANCY
82 years (2014)

ETHNIC GROUPS
Indigenous Swedish, Finnish, Sami; immigrant Danish, Greek, Norwegian, Turkish, Yugoslav

RELIGIOUS GROUPS
Lutheran (87 percent), Roman Catholic, Orthodox, Baptist, Muslim, Jewish, Buddhist, 13 percent (2014)

OFFICIAL LANGUAGE
Swedish

LITERACY RATE
99 percent

TIMELINE

IN SWEDEN	IN THE WORLD

12,000 BCE
Stone Age people settle Scandinavia.

753 BCE
Rome is founded.

400s CE
First Swedish state, Kingdom of the Svear, is established, centered in Uppland.

116–17 BCE
The Roman empire reaches its greatest extent, under Emperor Trajan (98–17).

550 CE
Gotlanders put themselves under the protection of the Swedish king.

600 CE
Height of Mayan civilization

800 CE
Beginning of the Viking Era

1000 CE
The Chinese perfect gunpowder and begin to use it in warfare.

1523
Gustav Eriksson Vasa is elected King of Sweden; Stockholm becomes the capital city.

1544
Vasa declares hereditary monarchy and Lutheranism as state religion.

1558–1603
Reign of Elizabeth I of England

1620
Pilgrims sail the Mayflower to America.

1776
U.S. Declaration of Independence

1818
Jean-Baptiste Bernadotte is crowned King Karl XIV.

1861
U.S. Civil War begins.

1875
A common basis of currency is established with Denmark and Norway.

1914
War in Europe begins; Sweden proclaims neutrality.

1914
World War I begins.

1939
World War II begins.

1944
All trade with Germany ceases.

IN SWEDEN	IN THE WORLD

1946
Sweden joins the United Nations.

1949
North Atlantic Treaty Organization (NATO) is formed.

1957
Russians launch Sputnik.

1965
Queen Louise dies.
Voting age is lowered from 21 to 20.

1966–69
Chinese Cultural Revolution

1973
Carl XVI Gustaf becomes king.

1975
Swedish parliament opens its 75th session.
Under the new constitution, the king is a figure-head with no real powers.

1982
Olof Palme is sworn in as prime minister.

1986
Palme is shot dead in Stockholm.

1991
Break-up of the Soviet Union

1995
Sweden joins the European Union. Visby enters the UNESCO World Heritage list.

1997
Britain returns Hong Kong to China.

2000
Öresund Bridge connecting Sweden and Denmark opens.

2001
9/11: Terrorists attack New York City and Washington, D.C.

2008
The U.S. elects first black president, Barack Obama

2009
The government reverses 30-year-old policy of phasing out nuclear power.

2011
Automaker Saab files for bankruptcy after failing to attract a buyer for the ailing business.

2014
Sweden wins 15 medals at Sochi Winter Olympics

2014
Egypt mediates Israel–Hamas cease-fire in deadly Gaza Strip hostilities

GLOSSARY

daghem (DAHG-hem)
A day-care center

Götaland (Yue-tah-land)
The region known as southern Sweden

gravad lax (GRAH-vahd lax)
Marinated salmon

gymnasium (gim-NAH-sium)
Senior high school

jojk (yoik)
A spontaneous, improvised style of singing

knäckebröd (ker-NECK-keh-brod)
Crispbread, sometimes called hard bread

lappkok (LAHP-shehk)
Reindeer marrow bone and liver broth

lingon (LING-gon)
A round, red berry, also called cowberry

lur (LOOR)
A wooden trumpet used for herding cattle

majstång (MAH-EE-stohng)
The maypole people dance around at midsummer

matjesill (MAHT-yeh-sill)
Sweet pickled herring

middag (MID-dahg)
The main meal of the day, served at 4 p.m.

Norrland (NOR-land)
The northern region of Sweden

ombudsman
An official investigating complaints against public authorities

Riksdag (RICKS-dahg)
Sweden's parliament

semlor (sehm-LOH)
A stuffed roll, usually eaten during Lent

skål (skohl)
A toast to one's health

smörgåsbord (SMOER-gos-bord)
A buffet of Swedish specialties

snaps (snahps)
Aquavit, a Swedish liquor made from fermented potatoes and barley

strömming (STROHM-ming)
A species of herring from the Baltic Sea

Svealand (SVEE-ah-land)
The region in central Sweden

tomte (TOM-teh)
Christmas gnome who brings gifts

FOR FURTHER INFORMATION

BOOKS

Cederlund, Johan, et al. *Anders Zorn: Sweden's Master Painter*. New York: Skira Rizzoli, 2013.

DK Publishing, *DK Eyewitness Travel Guide: Sweden*. New York: DK Travel, 2013.

Köster, Hans-Curt. *The World of Carl Larsson*. Iowa City: Penfield, 2003.

Larsson, Carl. *A Home: Paintings from a Bygone Age*. Edinburgh: Floris Books, 2006.

Lindgren, Astrid. *Pippi Longstocking*. Puffin Modern Classics. New York: Penguin, reissue 2005.

Lorenzen, Lily. *Of Swedish Ways*. New York: Harper Perennial, 1992.

Svenson, Charlotte Rosen, *CultureShock! Sweden*. Singapore: Marshall Cavendish, 2012.

DVDS/FILMS

Mamma Mia! The Movie (2008), Universal Studios; a musical comedy featuring the songs of ABBA.

Mother of Mine (2005), Film Movement (DVD 2007); WWII drama about Finnish children sent to neutral Sweden for safety.

My Life As a Dog (1985), Criterion (DVD 2003); Swedish coming-of-age drama by Lasse Hallström (rated PG-13).

The Seventh Seal (1957), Criterion (DVD 1999); Ingmar Bergman's classic allegory about man's search for meaning.

MUSIC

"The Best Loved Swedish Music and Folk Songs," Parlophone Sweden, 2007.

"Swedish Folk Tunes From Dalecarlia," Uppsala Cathedral Choir, Proprius, 2011.

WEBSITES

Government Offices of Sweden, www.government.se

Nobelprize.org, www.nobelprize.org

"The Sami—An Indigenous People in Sweden," www.samer.se/2137

Stockholm Business Region, www.visitstockholm.com/en

Sweden, sweden.se

Visit Sweden, www.visitsweden.com/sweden-us

Swedish Royal Court, www.kungahuset.se

BIBLIOGRAPHY

WEBSITES

BBC, Sweden profile, www.bbc.com/news/world-europe-17961621

CIA World Factbook, Sweden, www.cia.gov/library/publications/the-world-factbook/geos/sw.html

City of Stockholm, international.stockholm.se

Government Offices of Sweden, www.government.se

The Local, www.thelocal.se
www.thelocal.se/20140815/sweden-celebrates-200-years-of-peace

New York Times, "In Sweden, Men Can Have It All,"
www.nytimes.com/2010/06/10/world/europe/10iht-sweden.html?pagewanted=all&_r=0
_____,"Scandinavian Nonbelievers, Which Is Not to Say Atheists," www.nytimes.com/2009/02/28/us/28beliefs.html?pagewanted=all

Organization for Economic Cooperation and Development (OECD) Better Life Index, www.oecdbetterlifeindex.org/countries/sweden

ScienceNordic, "Increased divorce rates are linked to the welfare state,"
sciencenordic.com/increased-divorce-rates-are-linked-welfare-state

Sweden / Sverige, sweden.se

Swedish Environmental Protection Agency www.swedishepa.se

Swedish Ministry of Health and Social Affairs, "Ending Corporal Punishment," www.endcorporalpunishment.org/pages/pdfs/ending.pdf

Swedish Royal Court, www.kungahuset.se

U.S. State Department, "International Religious Freedom Report 2009: Sweden," www.state.gov/j/drl/rls/irf/2009/127339.htm

World Population Review, worldpopulationreview.com/countries/sweden-population

INDEX

INDEX